PRAISE FOR
"6 MONTHS TO 6 FIGURES"

"This is a MUST read for anybody wanting to elevate their results and income fast."

— **Scott Fay,** World Renown Business Coach, Vice President
John Maxwell Team, Author, Entrepreneur

"Peter gives us a blueprint and the tools to solidify your first 6 figure income, and explains in a very tactical and powerful way how to sustain it year after year"

— **Jordan Wirsz,** CEO SavantInvestments.com, top 40 under 40, nationally recognized Entrepreneur

"This book is missing one thing—hype. It's filled with real strategies and real techniques that will give you real results. If you want to set yourself up to make $100,000+ in the next six months, this is the #1 book to get you there."

— **Hal Elrod,** author of the #1 bestselling book,
The Miracle Morning (www.MiracleMorningBook.com)

"Do what's in this book! Peter will stir positive disruption in your entrepreneurial life by challenging you with practical wisdom needed to thrive in the new economy."

— **Isaac Tolpin,** CEO *ChooseGrowth.com*,
Co-Founder throwingboulders.com

"I love this book! If you're ready to achieve more than ever before and grow your business and yourself, then read and absorb the strategies in this brilliant book by my friend Peter Voogd! It's a game-changer!"

— **James Malinchak,** Featured on ABCs Hit TV Show,
Secret Millionaire, Author of the Top-Selling Book,
Millionaire Success Secrets Founder,
www.BigMoneySpeaker.com

"As a successful entrepreneur, speaker and author, Peter Voogd has walked the walk many times over. In his candid book "6 Months to 6 Figures," he gives clear and concise strategies that clear the path for those who strive to make a bigger impact. This is a must read for the dedicated and determined."

— **Dr. Tim Benson,** Harvard Medical School,
author of *Surviving Success,* drtimothybenson.com

6 MONTHS
To
6 FIGURES

*"The Fastest Way to Get From Where You Are to
Where You Want to Be, Regardless of the Economy."*

ISBN PAPERBACK: 978-0-9909973-0-6

ISBN HARDCOVER: 978-0-9909973-1-3

Cover design: Hugo Fernandez, JD Media Productions.
Interior design: Hugo Fernandez, JD Media Productions.
Editing: Kelly Stokes Brown, KSB Marketing Message.

Printed in the USA

The information presented herein represents the view of the author as of the date of publication. This book is presented for informational purposes only. Due to the rate at which conditions change, the author reserves the right to alter and update his opinions based on new conditions. While every attempt has been made to verify the information in this book, neither the author nor his affiliates/partners assume any responsibility for errors, inaccuracies, or omissions.

This book is being given to:

_____

Because I care about you and your greater success.

Game Changers Academy:
The Elite Mastermind Community
For Entrepreneurs

You talked. We listened. I'm blessed to say that over 250,000 people all around the world have now read this book.

After we started getting hundreds of success stories as a direct result of utilizing the content in this book, we knew we had to do more.

So, we did.

To find out more about our exclusive *Game Changers Academy* masterclass program and community, please visit:

www.GameChangersMovement.com

TABLE OF CONTENTS

ABOUT THE AUTHOR:
PETER VOOGD

 A visionary, game changer, speaker, author, mentor, and dedicated entrepreneur, Peter Voogd is on a mission to shift our culture, and won't stop until his vision becomes a reality. Peter can't stand traditional education, and feels our society isn't doing enough to educate, teach, and train our youth on how to REALLY thrive in this tough economy. He's taken it upon himself to guide and educate our Millennials on what it takes to not only succeed, but THRIVE! Peter's strategies have been featured in *Entrepreneur Magazine, Forbes, Huffington Post, Business Insider, Yahoo Small Business, Yahoo Finance, MSN,* SUCCESS and many other international publications.

Peter has seen a lot of success over the years, but even more failure. He's used his past to design his ideal future, and has dedicated the last 10 years to helping people maximize their potential. He's been labeled as the leading authority for Millennials and one of the top influencers to follow along with Tony Robbins, Gary Vaynerchuk and more. He has an authentic, raw understanding of what it takes to motivate and inspire. He's trained and led over 6,000 Entrepreneurs, Sales Professionals, Managers, College Students, Young Professionals, Business Owners, Olympians and many others to high levels of success.

He started his first business when he was 15, and found himself broke, stressed and discouraged by the age of 22. By 23, he had made his first 6-figure income, and 3 1/2 years later his earnings were over $1 million. He then took the same formula and applied it in another industry, and has dedicated himself to teaching it to others so they don't make the same mistakes he did. Despite the challenge of lacking training, Peter became the fastest manager to reach $1 million in annual sales in his company's 60 + year history, but left his 6 figure income because the magnitude of his mission was growing. He strongly believes the more people you help to succeed, the more successful you become.

Peter has started a few movements to empower and train entrepreneurs and young professionals called *The Game Changers Academy* as well as the program driven from this book, *6 Months to 6 Figures* (see more at www.PeterJVoogd.com). Both have quickly become some of the most prestigious training and networking communities in the world, and continue to attract ambitious professionals and entrepreneurs from all over the world. He understands on a deep level that entrepreneurs are the driving force and future of our society.

He is also the Founder of one of iTunes top podcasts, "*The Young Entrepreneur Lifestyle Podcast,*" which is focused on bringing results, guidance, and excellence to entrepreneurs worldwide. It's helping entrepreneurs do business and live life on their terms.

Learn more at: www.peterjvoogd.com/podcast

Connect with Peter on social media:

Facebook	:	PeterJVoogd
LinkedIn	:	Peter Voogd
Twitter	:	PeterVoogd23
Instagram	:	PeterJVoogd
Snapchat	:	Ambition23
Google+	:	Peter Voogd
Email	:	Peter@PeterJVoogd.com
Facebook Group	:	Facebook.com/groups/ SixMonthsToSixFigures

FREE ACTION GUIDE & BONUS RESOURCES

This book is meant to inspire you to get results like it has for thousands of others. How does it do that? By getting you into motion. You will see many action items throughout the book and I encourage you to take these very seriously.

Trust me: They work!

As a thank you for purchasing *6 Months to 6 Figures* and committing yourself to excellence, building a business that matters, and taking control of your future, I've assembled a series of valuable tools you can use to help maximize your entrepreneurial experience.

Sure, I could have offered you some BS special report or free video seminar like most 'online marketers,' but I'd rather give you something practical that will help you move your business forward and get you on the path to making immediate income.

Here is just part of what you can get instant access to:

- Your *6 Figures in 6 Months* Blueprint Action Guide
- Productivity Excellence Blueprint and exclusive MP3
- Plus My Elite '6X Strategy' Training

... For FREE. That's $785 worth of book bonus.

Take action and download the free PDFs, audio and training at:

www.PeterJVoogd.com/bonuses

INTRODUCTION

I assure you this book will not be like anything you've ever read, and I'm going to talk about things in a way you may have never heard before. I might say things that will rub you the wrong way, make you mad, make you question your past beliefs, and interrupt your normal thought patterns. GOOD.

Sometimes, the things you don't want to hear are the things you need to hear the most. Although good friends are a big part of life, I didn't create this book to become your friend; I created it to help you improve the most important areas of your life and business. I created it to help you live a better lifestyle. I created it to help you thrive as an entrepreneur, sales professional, and leader. The worst thing in life is regret, and if I can help you elevate your results, live a more fulfilled life, and lower your regret, I've done my job. I want to make a bold promise. I can assure you with great confidence that this book will create real change for you, and, more importantly, move your life, business, and results forward.

Here's the catch: YOU must take action. It's been said that, after seminars and conferences, only 5% actually use what they've learned. Why is that? It's because inspiration is very short term; it feels good in the moment but doesn't last past the activity producing it. In this book, we focus on shifting habits, gaining better perspective, and interrupting bad thought patterns instead of just supplying inspiration. I've realized that the biggest inspiration of all is seeing progress and results, which comes from new habits. When you begin the formation of a new habit, stick to it, and see the lasting change in your newfound life.

This book is an attempt at a fresh and practical perspective on the wealth of knowledge available about how to be a successful entrepreneur. As I developed as a young entrepreneur, and experienced challenges and successes, I realized very few books offered the kind of success advice I now give to those I mentor. By telling my personal stories and relating them to those of other successful entrepreneurs, I set out to create a book that focuses on the core principles needed to teach entrepreneurs what they may not find in schools, magazines, or online. Furthermore, my goal in writing this book is to help young entrepreneurs avoid the mistakes I've made. Mistakes during early years of a business can be extremely harmful.

Here is what you must understand: *everything* has changed. What it took to succeed five to ten years ago doesn't work anymore, and some say it's become the toughest time in human history for young entrepreneurs, sales professionals, students and youth to succeed. Hear me out. There are constant distractions, evolving technology, information overload, entitlement mindsets, and minimal real guidance. This is creating frustration, overwhelm, and consistent stress for those wanting to succeed and escape the herd of mediocrity. According to Forbes.com, 71% of people hate what they do, and are actively disengaged at work. According to *The Huffington Post*, the average price of college is up 27% while the average income a student makes when graduating is at an all-time low. 60% of college students can't find work in their field after graduation, while leaving school on average with $35,200 in debt (CNN.com). Yikes. This doesn't give our youth much hope...

Or does it?...

The need for real leadership is increasing minute-by-minute, and I have become frustrated watching so many people waste their potential because of lack of guidance, being sold the wrong plan, or given false expectations of success. Don't get me wrong; I've made every mistake in the world when it comes to entrepreneurship, business, and life in general. I wish I had a book like this as I was coming up in the entrepreneurship and business world. It would have saved me hundreds of hours of headache, stress, and uncertainty, along with thousands of dollars! People say you need to learn from experience. I say that's too expensive. You must learn from other people's experience and don't repeat those same mistakes. Isn't that more intelligent?

Now for the good news: Yes, there is a lot of good news in the midst of our "economic crisis"... You just need an open mind and the right perspective to see it. Tony Robbins, who has had a tremendous impact on my life, stated:

> *"There is maximum profit and opportunity in maximum fear and pessimism."*

There are endless possibilities, and more opportunities than you could even imagine for those committed to self-improvement. 68% of the Fortune 500 companies were started in a depression or a recession. Some of the companies our country was founded on were built and created in some of the toughest of times. I want you to pay close attention and take seriously what I'm about to say. This is the best opportunity in human history to create the life you want; a life full of income, abundance, influence, and flexibility. Now, just because there are opportunities doesn't mean it's easy to make the most of them. You need to know a couple of important things first, and in this book I want to give you everything you need to become the best at what you do, and achieve more than you ever thought possible. These aren't philosophies or theories I've read in a book, or learned in a business class. Yes, I've taken many business classes from a very well known business school, but the "theories" I learned didn't help me much when I was in the field running a business. They are a result of being in business since I was 15, being in the trenches, going broke, making over a million dollars before the age of 26, massive struggle, frustration, depression, anxiety, mentorship, and consistently persevering past all obstacles. The skills, ideas, and tools I'll share with you are the same ones that have helped me create an exceptional lifestyle for myself, and for those I work with.

As I'm writing this, I am on a plane from Hawaii to San Diego, and the day after I get home, I'm leaving for an event in Newport Beach. Then two weeks later, I'm flying to Las Vegas for a couple days to meet with two of my mentors. A couple days after that, I am speaking at an event in LA called "Limitless" put on by amazing entrepreneur, Chris Cooper. From Los Angeles, my girlfriend and I are going on a three-week road trip up to Oregon. I then fly to New York City for an event called Entrepreneur Organization (EO) with my good friend Hal Elrod. I get back on a Thursday, and leave the next morning for a trip to Puerto Vallarta with my family … a surprise I'm creating for them. Two weeks later, I am coming back to Hawaii for two weeks to speak to an amazing group of young entrepreneurs, and will be working from my iPhone and laptop the entire time. This is just the next two months, and this is all while running multiple businesses. I know this isn't the typical lifestyle most people live, but I know you're reading this book because you don't want the life most people have. I didn't either, and I encourage you to take the road less traveled. You want to live an inspiring and world-class life. I'm here to show you how.

I heard once from a mentor of mine:

> *"A real leader isn't somebody who develops the most followers; a real leader is somebody who develops the most leaders."*

I pride myself more in the lifestyles and increased results I've helped thousands achieve. That's a lot more rewarding to me than doing it myself, but in order to help others you must help yourself first. I know coaches, mentors, and entrepreneurs who are struggling themselves, but trying to help others become successful. That doesn't work out very well. So lets get started with creating your first 6-figure income. If you've already created a 6 figure net income, then focus on your first 7-figure income. Here's why this is important:

The US Census Bureau Document S1901, entitled INCOME IN THE PAST 12 MONTHS, found that less than 20% of families make over $100,000 and less than 8% make over $150,000. Due to increases in the cost of living, a person would need to make $172,103 today in order to have the same purchasing power as someone making $100,000 in 1990. $100,000 isn't what it use to be, but it's a great start, and enough to break away from the majority.

This book is about YOU. Your results. Your future. Your income. Your story. I won't take up too much time talking about myself, however, I do want you to know who I am, why I can help you, and how this book came about.

My parents wisely moved my brother and me from Oakland, California to a small town on the Oregon coast, a retirement community with around 7,000 people. I wouldn't exactly call this town "the city of dreams." From an early age, I knew I didn't want to go the hard labor route, although that's what most people in my town did. I tried to get out of everything I possibly could involving work or manual labor. Ironic, because my dad had been in construction, and my brother didn't mind it. Now don't get me wrong, there is nothing wrong with working in construction, I just learned I would rather be the guy running the company than doing the labor.

My dad, who recognized this about me told me to, "Use your brains, not your hands." I got introduced to eBay when I was 15, and started selling shoes from my mom's office immediately after learning I could. I eventually sold bigger items, and would buy in bulk and sell individually. The fact that I could put something online and sell it to somebody in a different state was mind blowing to me at the time. I was hooked, and that was the first experience with entrepreneurship.

I'm often asked what made the difference in my early years. Why didn't I choose the normal route and do what everybody else was doing? When I think back, there have been three big turning points that guided the trajectory of my life.

Turning Point 1: Growing up, a couple of my friends worked for my dad in construction, and I remember one day when my friends were piling sand in a bucket for my dad all day. I tried it and got half way down the hill and told my dad I had something I had to do so I couldn't finish. I laugh now because I know my dad isn't dumb. He just knew I wanted to get out of the hard labor and figured it wasn't worth arguing.

I wanted to see how my shoes were doing on eBay. To my surprise, I had made $91 dollars. I then immediately calculated how much my friend made working 8 hours with my dad, and it was $63. My 15-year-old mind was confused. I just made a $91 profit on eBay, and it took me only 15 minutes and no physical labor. My friend worked his butt off for eight hours and made only $63? *"I am never getting a normal job,"* I thought to myself. Here's what I realized years later, and it must be understood by you now. I didn't get paid for just posting on eBay.

I got paid for the courage to think differently and take a risk.

That opened up a whole new way of thinking and introduced me to entrepreneurship, which saved my life. Up to that point, I felt like an outcast. I could not pay attention in class, I rebelled against those trying to control me, and I couldn't stand people putting a label on me. I had a taste of what was possible, and that's all I needed.

Turning Point 2: I went against my gut and got a 'normal' hourly wage job, mainly because I was told so many times I needed a normal job to get experience. Side note: NEVER let other people's opinion of you persuade your decisions. However, I did, and got a job working as a valet at a local casino. As you could guess, I didn't last long. I would show up early, go out of my way to help customers, and even got a letter written to my manager about my customer service and 'extra mile' attitude. Regardless of what I did, my paychecks stayed the same. I had a co-worker who had been there a little longer than me. He would do bare minimum work, steal customers from my co-worker and I, and had a horrible attitude. He was getting paid more than my friend and me, and it didn't make any logical sense in my mind. I went the extra mile, I helped more customers, I added more value to the casino, but he got paid more?

My tipping point: I remember very vividly sitting in the valet booth, leaning back in my chair and thinking, "I should add up my paychecks for the entire summer and see how much I am going to make." I did exactly that.

$7.05 * 30 hours – taxes = $147 * 14 weeks (summer) = $2,058

Regardless of how hard I worked, no matter how much value or business I brought to the casino, I would make that exact amount. No matter what my potential was, or how ambitious I acted, it meant nothing to my pay. It was the most de-motivating thing I've ever experienced. I stuck it out over the summer with plans to never work an hourly job again. I don't regret getting a normal job because it re-enforced to me that the entrepreneur route was the right choice for me.

You're either building your dreams, or helping someone else build theirs. I once heard the acronym JOB stands for *Just Over Broke,* and realized most people I was around who had typical 'jobs' always complained about their boss, money, time off, being tired, or not wanting to work, and I was convinced I didn't want to live like that. I wanted a lifestyle I was proud to live. I didn't want my potential in somebody else's hands, and I definitely didn't want somebody else to tell me what I was worth. There are endless ways to validate working an hourly job you don't thoroughly enjoy, but please don't. I'm sure I'll get some haters for not promoting minimum wage jobs, but I want to challenge you to think bigger and bolder. It's okay to start this way, and great if it's your dream job, but most of the time it's not.

Turning Point 3: Reading the book *Rich Dad Poor Dad* by Robert Kiyosaki gave me a whole new perspective on life and business. It validated everything I had been telling my parents. My mom would say to me, "You need to start with a normal job and work your way up like everybody else." I'd reply, "I don't want to be like everybody else! Everybody else hates what they do, complains about money, and prays for weekends."

I love what Seth Godin says:

> *"Instead of wondering when your next vacation is, maybe you should set up a life you don't need to escape from."*

I wanted to design my future; I wanted my income to be based on my hustle, work ethic, and potential. Not my age, time spent on the job, or what others thought I was worth. This book taught me a couple of life-changing philosophies that guided my decisions from that moment on. Our society has low standards for people and for achieving real wealth. One in three Americans believe their best chance of becoming wealthy is winning the lottery. Are you kidding me? Here are the cliff notes from *Rich Dad Poor Dad* and some of my favorite takeaways:

The book was about two dads teaching their sons two very different philosophies. One had a college degree and the other had an eighth grade education. The rich dad wasn't rich yet, and poor dad wasn't poor yet as they were both just starting out. Both dads were struggling with money, and each family had different views. One said, "Love of money is the root of all evil," the other said, "Lack of money is the root of all evil." Both fathers influenced their sons and it was hard to know which father to follow because they both said such different things. One said, "I can't afford it," the other insisted on saying, "How can I afford it?" One is a statement, one a question; one lets you off the hook, and one makes you think. Exercising your brain makes it stronger. The stronger it is, the more money it makes.

One of the reasons the rich get richer, the poor get poorer, and the middle class stays middle class is because the subject of money is taught at home and not in school. What can a poor parent tell their child about money? Sadly, bad philosophies are all they know and is why they are where they are. Money is not taught in school. Schools equal scholastic, not finance. This explains how most bankers and accountants, who are so smart, struggle financially all their life. Behind that saying, "I can't become wealthy . . ." is mental laziness. Proper physical exercise enhances health. Proper mental exercise increases wealth. Laziness decreases both health and wealth—if you're lazy physically, then you're lazy mentally. Either you work for money, or money works for you. Just hearing that shifted my perspective, as I want it to shift yours. If you haven't read the book *Rich Dad Poor Dad*, it's a must-read.

Some jobs are great, and perfect for the person doing it. Some people have their dream jobs, and I'm not downplaying jobs. I am saying you were put on this earth to express your creative genius, play to your strengths, and to do big things. There are certain jobs that will not permit you to create a six-figure income, and I want to create proper expectations before you take any further action. Here are a couple questions you must ask yourself to make sure you're in a position to create your first six, and eventually, seven-figure income. I realized I couldn't get to a six-figure income doing more of what got me five figures.

- Are there people in your same field or position currently making a 6 figure income? How long have they been there?
- Do you have the capability to do it faster?
- Is your income capped, or do you have the capability to make as much as you'd like?

If you're currently in a position you hate, in a position that doesn't play to your talents and gifts, and you're trying to figure out what's next for you, this book will help. Let me ask you a couple questions first.

- How serious are you about building your dreams?

- How serious are you about living an exceptional lifestyle?

- How serious are you about creating your first six-figure income?

I want you to pull out your calendar, and fast forward six months from now and mark that as the day you'll leave your current position. I talk to people all the time who have tentative plans to leave their "corporate" job or the job they don't enjoy. I ask them the date they are leaving and they say they have no idea. The date makes it real. Six months is enough time to craft the perfect plan, develop the skills you need to start your journey towards real success, and gain clarity towards your next venture. I'm here for you, and have helped many people leave their 'jobs', and create or design their dream opportunity. There is only one real success, to be able to live your life your way on your terms. I'm not saying it will be easy, I'm saying it's worth it. Embrace those tough times, because that's when your real hunger for success is developed.

1

THE HIDDEN OPPORTUNITY

"When we are no longer able to change the situation,
we are challenged to change ourselves."

— Victor Frankl

Your life is formed by the perspectives and philosophies you adopt, and changing your perspective can create an immediate shift in your life and business. Have you ever thought about what experiences have shaped the direction of your life? Doing so can change the game for you, as it did for me. I hope to strengthen your perspective on what it really takes to succeed in this new economy. Don't be fooled. The rules you've been taught don't apply anymore. Everything has changed, and it's adapt or die in this new economy. I want you to learn from my toughest failures, and my greatest successes. Most people haven't put much thought into why they aren't really thriving as they could, or the real reasons they are where they are.

One of the greatest philosophies I've learned, which has had an immense impact on my results, was from business philosopher,

Jim Rohn. This principle goes against the mold of what schools teach, how most are raised and brought up, and what media portrays to society. If you understand this powerful philosophy and implement it into your life, you will develop a substantial advantage over those who don't. If this is your first time hearing this philosophy, then I assure you this will forever change your perspective on success, as it did mine.

Jim Rohn stated in one of his early seminars…

> *"You get paid for bringing value to the marketplace, and if you're not very valuable you don't make much money."*

This was an eye-opener for me because I realized I wasn't doing much to become more valuable, and I wasn't making money either. People tend to complain about the economy, their job, the government, their lack of income, but aren't doing much to improve their value or skills. The harsh reality we all must understand is that you will always be paid exactly what you are worth, or believe you are worth. If somebody is making minimum wage, that is the value they're bringing to the marketplace. Why would somebody make $500 an hour, and somebody else make $15 an hour? It's quite simple. One has become more valuable to the marketplace than the other. If you're not very valuable to the marketplace you don't get much money. The quicker you understand this, the quicker you can advance in this fast paced and evolving economy.

Here is the Major Problem

Time on a job or years at a specific occupation does not increase the inherent value of that job being done. In most cases, after the first few years, it doesn't increase the value of the employees either. You often hear people say, "I have 20 years of experience, I should get paid more!" But in actuality, that person has one year of experience repeated 20 times. If they're not sharpening their skills, learning better tools, or constantly trying to better themselves, they aren't becoming more valuable. Why should they expect more money? Age doesn't guarantee a higher income. Value does.

People don't get more valuable hanging around for years; age isn't value. You see, most people want more money, but aren't willing to do anything that delivers more value to that business or their customers. Jim Rohn says:

> *"Don't bring your needs to the marketplace,*
> *bring your skills."*

What he was telling us is that we get paid for the value that we bring to other people's lives, not what we want or think we need. Success doesn't respond to want or need, it responds to deserve.

Skills are valuable, needs are not. You might have a desperate need for money to pay for medical bills to help cure a sick child; but as desperate as that child might be, and as sincere as your desire to help might be, what you want doesn't add any *value* to YOU personally, and doesn't offer any value to the marketplace. In turn, the marketplace is unlikely to reward you with the money that you need. Jim Rohn also states, "If you don't feel well, tell your doctor, but not the marketplace." The marketplace is only interested in what you can do that is of value. The fact that you don't feel well is nothing more than a lame excuse. The marketplace is not interested in excuses—it just wants results and real value from you. He's telling us not to ask for anything without offering something in return. What does the marketplace want? Value for money. I've helped many young entrepreneurs create their first six- figure income. I've personally helped 19-year-olds make over $15,000 in two weeks, and I've been mentored by somebody who made their first million by age 21. I've also met numerous people who complain they aren't making enough money. They all have the same opportunity, yet some thrive and some don't. Why? Different perspectives.

The Secret

> *"Learn to work harder on yourself than you do on your job. If you work hard on your job you can make a living, but if you work hard on yourself you'll make a fortune."*
> — Jim Rohn

When I heard this, a lightbulb went off in my head. The earlier you realize and adopt this powerful philosophy, the sooner you'll become successful. You don't need to go to work on the economy, you don't need to change your company, the government, your boss, or your circumstances. You need to go to work on yourself. If you change, everything will change for you. You may change companies, you might change tactics, strategies or mentors... but YOU are always the constant, and you will still be there. Strive to become a better person, and, instead of comparing yourself to others, differentiate. The goal is to be slightly better than who you were the day before. The only person you should try to be better than is the person you were yesterday.

The Value Of Time

> *"Time is more valuable than money. You can always get more money, but you can never get more time."*

Is it possible to become twice as valuable to the marketplace, and make twice as much money in the same amount of time? Of course it is. There is nothing more valuable than time invested wisely and intentionally. You can sow your time and get anything you want. You can sow your time and increase your circle of influence, make more money, or increase your health. Nothing is more priceless than time, so never waste this precious gift. It takes time to bring value to the marketplace, but we get paid for the *value*, not the time. So it's what you do with your time that really matters. I've never met a rich man who didn't value his time, and I've never met a poor man who did. Learn to see the value of *time*. because with time, anything can be accomplished. I often laugh at those who hate on successful people when they have the same 24 hours in a day and the same opportunities.

If you want to take your business or income to the next level, you need to make growth a part of your daily agenda. Do something that increases the value you bring to your business, your work, your clients or customers. It's not very complicated to change your current income level. You simply need to offer more value to the marketplace.

So how do you bring 'value' to the marketplace? By becoming better at everything you do. I often tell my sales force their goal should be to become irreplaceable, and to become so good at what they do that people can't ignore them. If you consistently build your character, skills, and value to others, you will quickly advance in the game of economics.

Here are places where you will reliably find opportunities to increase your value and stand out against your competition.

Expertise: Study your industry, learn from your competitors.

Productivity: What and how much you get done.

Efficiency: How you get done what you get done.

Multiplication: Getting things done by means other than manual labor.

Influence: What you can persuade others to get done.

Celebrity Status: How well you are known by your target audience.

Reputation: What others know and think about you.

Vision: What you see that others don't.

Personality: How you treat others and how well you connect.

Attitude: Your attitude toward yourself and toward others.

Awareness: Knowing your strengths and what you're the best at.

Masterminding: Surrounding yourself with those you can learn from.

There are no limits to your success as an entrepreneur when you commit to growing and becoming more valuable. You are always in control of your economy regardless of your outside circumstances. In order to make room for your gifts, you must follow the steps outlined in this book, which will enable you to work on your skills, develop new disciplines, and thoroughly increase your value.

CHAPTER

2

MASTERY VS. INFORMATION OVERLOAD

"Amateurs practice until they get it right; professionals practice until they can't get it wrong."

— Unknown

There is more content online than ever before, and there is a wave sweeping our society, especially millennials, of overwhelm and information overload. There are videos, books, seminars, training programs, and advice coming from every direction on thousands of different topics. The overload of information is making it extremely challenging to master anything, and when you're overwhelmed you seek out distractions. The mastery concept helped me early in my career and was a huge part of my first six-figure income. I call it the *Mastery vs. Overload Principle.*

Yes, to build wealth you first must build a wealth of knowledge. You need new information, new wisdom, and new ideas to take your business to a new level, but the power lies in how fast you can implement the right information into your daily routines. The right information is only part of the equation. The real power lies in implementation.

Mastery is one of the highest forms of performance and success. The only way to become successful is to master the fundamentals, but the fundamentals you adopt must be congruent to your end results and goals. Most people have so much information - they read books, they go to conferences and seminars, they watch all the free videos online - but they aren't intentional, so they get overwhelmed and become paralyzed. The immature learner wants to get as much information as he can as fast as he can, but you'll usually find him broke, stressed, and lacking real clarity. The mature learner is very deliberate with what he studies and what he puts to mind. Achievers focus on listening to something until they've adopted it into their daily agenda and have experienced increased results. Once they've seen progress, they move on to the next skill.

Wanting to learn more when you haven't mastered the current information is a huge reason most stay broke and stressed. Mastering new skills is not optional in today's business environment and changing economy. In our fast-moving, competitive world, being able to learn new skills is crucial for success and achievement. It's not enough to be smart—you need to always be getting smarter, and if you're not moving forward, you're falling behind. It's more about focus than intelligence. I know a lot of brilliant people who haven't accomplished anything or used their knowledge at all. I also know numerous millionaires who aren't that intelligent, but have tremendous work ethic and hustle! Knowledge is not power. It's what you do with what you know that leads to mastery. Action is the only thing that will ultimately determine your success. Unapplied knowledge is useless. The only way to hit those big goals you dream about is to grow into them, and make sure you're intentional in all you do. Mastery is a new form of learning and I challenge you to adopt it into your current lifestyle. Here are a couple of keys in getting started:

Start Small: Self-improvement can feel overwhelming. Realize you can't take on everything. If you do, you'll never accomplish anything. Instead, choose one or two skills to focus on at a time, and break that skill or skills down into manageable goals. Throughout this book, I ask questions and give you action steps to take. First, you will define your goals and priorities so you have clarity on what you're aiming to achieve.

> *"If you have more than three priorities,*
> *you don't have any."*
> — Jim Collins

Reflect Along The Way: To move from experimentation to mastery, you need to reflect on what you're learning. Otherwise, the new skill won't stick, and you'll fall back into overload. Reflecting on and talking about your progress helps you get valuable feedback, keeps you accountable, and cements the change. I often hear people talking about how many books they've read and bragging about their goal of 50 books this year. I respect their desire to grow, but I'd rather master three to five books that are congruent and in alignment with my goals than read 50 I can't apply to my business or life.

Challenge Yourself to Teach it to Others: One of the quickest ways to learn something new and to practice it is to teach others how to do it. Share what you learn with your team, your managers, your co-workers, or even your customers. When reading a new book, I don't move on to the next chapter until I feel I could teach the chapter I just read. Most people forget what they've read an hour after they've read it and it doesn't help them advance towards the goals they've defined. What's the point of reading if it doesn't sharpen your perspective, improve your results, or help your legacy?

Be patient: Too often, we approach a new skill with the attitude that we should nail it right out of the gate. The reality is that it takes much longer. It's not going to happen overnight. It usually takes six months or more to develop a new skill, and it may take longer for others to see and appreciate it. People around you will only notice 10% of every 100% change you make.

From this point on, I want you be more intentional with what you study, read, or listen to. Make sure it's congruent with your weekly, monthly, and yearly goals. I'll explain in a later chapter how to take full advantage of this philosophy. The simple act of being more intentional with what you study can set you apart from those around you, and successful people are always looking for ways to differentiate themselves. Sadly, most people will operate on information overload instead of mastery, and continue to be overwhelmed. Or even worse, they learn just enough to get by and stop learning. Apple said it bluntly...

> *"We shouldn't be criticized for using Chinese workers. The U.S. has stopped producing people with the skills we need."*

Ouch! When I say develop yourself, grow, and improve your skills, I don't mean traditional schooling. School sometimes distracts you from the things that actually matter in advancing your career and life. Weird, but true. Take self-made billionaire Warren Buffet's advice:

> *"The best education you can get is investing in yourself, and that doesn't mean college or university."*

Your education doesn't end at graduation. It begins. The sooner you realize that all the skills you need to learn to succeed will occur after you leave the confines of educational institutions, the sooner you will succeed. Let others overload themselves with information while you commit to mastery.

CHAPTER

3

MONEY MATTERS

"Money isn't everything, but it's right
up there with oxygen."

— Zig Ziglar

Now that you've learned the power of mastery versus overload, I want to get into one of the most important topics you can master. Money. It's a topic rarely discussed, and one of the main reasons most people don't have enough. What's enough? Well, that's up to you. Have you ever noticed that it's usually those who claim they don't care about money who are broke? I personally know what it's like to have nothing, to stress about paying my next bill, and to feel hopeless. I also know what it's like to thrive, and I've been fortunate in creating some great income as well. The topic of wealth, income, and money making in general is often discussed or viewed in a negative light. I'm sure there will be people who will not approve of the title of this book, because it talks about making money. Why not get wealthy? Why not become a millionaire? Why not focus on making as much money as you can? I did an experiment not too long ago, and I tried living life with no money. I

21

also lived with a lot of it. I found out having money was a lot more enjoyable, fulfilling, exciting, and gave me more choices. It also helped me expand my reach and spread my message to a bigger audience. As my friend Grant Cardone says, *"Poor doesn't make any sense."* Eliminate any and all ideas that being poor is somehow okay. As Bill Gates said, *"If you're born poor, it's not your mistake. But if you die poor, it is your mistake."*

Have you ever heard anybody say any of these?

"Money is the root of all evil."

"Rich people are greedy."

"Money won't make you happy."

"You don't want to be one of *those* people."

All these phrases are usually said by those who lack financial freedom and intelligence. Our society is afraid of being labeled as greedy or money hungry, but what must be understood is that money is a crucial part of freedom. Now, I will tell you money is an excellent servant, but a terrible master. If you're only driven by money, it makes it difficult to build a lifestyle and live life on your terms. So you must do both, make money and live life on your terms, which is what I'm here to teach you.

It's so easy to get caught up in the day to day grind, and to forget about the vision of abundance and prosperity. How can we focus on building wealth when we're barely getting by? How can we focus on financial freedom when we're two paychecks away from going broke? Sadly, these are common questions in today's society. If you want to break free of mediocrity, you must change your perspective on wealth and understand what it really takes to create wealth. I'm not just talking action and habits here. I'm talking more about the mindset critical for your success. This book will give you all the answers you need and hopefully inspire you to change your habits and perspective of what's truly possible for you, your family, and the legacy you're leaving behind.

Thomas Stanley has been studying wealth for years and has done numerous studies and research. He discovered that there are only four groups of people:

3% Are Wealthy — Those are people with $2 million in investable assets. Some people are house rich, but cash poor. This refers to people who have $2 million to invest.

27% Are Financially Comfortable — To me, you own a reasonably successful business or you've got a very stable job. You either own your home outright or have a very manageable mortgage. You could go out and buy a new car without needing a loan. You could afford to take a year off from work to pursue a dream and not return mired in debt. If you're half of a couple, you could live well enough if either of you stopped working.

55% Are Living Paycheck to Paycheck — This classification is fairly easy to attain. Just spend more than you make. Most people are putting a lot of their expenses on their credit cards. Most spend all of their money on things that have nothing to do with their future. That's why they will NEVER advance. I would define this as anyone who couldn't skip more than two paychecks without sinking further into debt. They're probably debt-slaves as it is, or maybe their expenses are high because they have a lot of kids, an expensive medical condition, or just graduated college themselves. You most likely will not find this group investing in themselves.

15% Are Further In Debtors — They don't just live paycheck to paycheck; they go further into debt monthly. 70% of the population are either living paycheck to paycheck or getting further in debt every month.

My goal is to help you reach that top 30%, and the younger you understand how to get there, the sooner you'll get there. You must first realize it's not the money that will solve your problems. If people think money solves problems, I am afraid those people will have a rough ride. Intelligence solves problems and produces money. Personal growth solves problems. Money without financial intelligence is money soon gone.

I want to deal in reality and I want to create proper expectations for you. If you're working at an hourly job making $10 per hour, it would take you working 29 hours a day, 365 days a year to create a six-figure income. That's obviously not possible. If you're working for $20 per hour, you would still have to work 14.5 hrs a day for 365 days to create your first six-figure income. You would have to make $48.00 per hour and work 40 hours a week with no vacation time. I don't know a single person who wants that, and I challenge you to expect more from yourself than anybody else expects of you.

This book is for those who have the entrepreneur mindset, aspire to become an entrepreneur, or just want to create an amazing lifestyle. I define an entrepreneur as somebody who controls their income and makes money through their intelligence, relationships, ideas, and implementation. Entrepreneurs don't want to play it safe. Entrepreneurs take risks. Entrepreneurs include sales professionals, network marketers, business owners, leaders, speakers, authors, coaches, and those working for themselves. Can you work nine to five and become an entrepreneur on the side? Absolutely. I believe everybody should experience entrepreneurship at some point in their life.

You need four things to build a great future and fully enjoy what you do. You'll know if you're in the right spot if your business meets this criteria. If it doesn't, it's your responsibility to create your ideal lifestyle, nobody else's. I can assure you that lifestyle, legacy, and loving what you do are more important than income, but it takes income to make that happen. Here are the "*4 W's to Lifestyle Satisfaction,*" created by Michael Masterson, best-selling author and successful entrepreneur:

The 4 W's to Lifestyle Satisfaction:

What do you do? — What's the possibility and upside? Is the opportunity endless? Is it something you enjoy doing? Does it really inspire and help people? Are you in 100% control of your schedule, income, and advancement? Most people say they love what they do, but deep down, if they could do anything they wanted, they would do something else. Please don't settle. If you REALLY love what you do, you'll never work a day in your life.

Who do you do it with? — Who is leading you? Are they inspiring, and do they challenge you? The times I've thrived the most were because of the mentors and leaders guiding me. They lived the lifestyle I wanted, they had the amazing relationships I wanted, and they practiced what they preached. Do you love and appreciate those you associate with daily? Most people hate what they do, hate their boss, and hate their co-workers. Life is too short to have toxic people around you.

When you do it, and when you don't? — Do you have flexibility? Can you design your business to fit around your lifestyle? Ultimately, you are in control of your own future and can take it as big and as far as you want to grow. You need the real passion to pull your potential out. Are you up before your alarm because you're so excited to take on your day or do you sleep in, dreading getting up? Gary Vaynerchuk told me if you hate what you do, even a small percentage, it's time for a change.

Where do you work? — Can you work from home or while you're traveling? Can you move if you're tired of where you are living? Do you have an inspiring environment that sparks your creativity and genius? This is why becoming a lifestyle entrepreneur is becoming the "American dream."

I am confidently guessing you have goals to increase your

income. Maybe you're sick of making the same income or you can't stand the feeling of struggling financially. I can relate. What is the difference between those who are thriving and those who aren't? Well, we all have the same twenty-four hours in a day, so they must be doing something different with their time, right? They must have a better perspective about money and how it's earned. If you are not satisfied with your income, let me give you some straight-forward tactical tips that can be used right away.

Stop doing what you're doing: The first thing you must do if you are dissatisfied is stop doing what you've been doing, because that's what created your current reality. We've all heard the famous quote by Albert Einstein, "Insanity is doing the same thing over and over and expecting a different result." What's great about life and opportunity is the chance to completely change the story and direction overnight. Regardless of your past decisions, you're always one decision away from making the right one.

Don't let money define you: Your self-worth has nothing to do with your finances. Whether you have a negative bank account or $10 million, your confidence should never waiver. If anything, your confidence should increase when you are stressed, and this stress should motivate you to NEVER feel that way again. Being wealthy is a state of mind, but so is being broke. Who you are defines you, not what you possess. (More about confidence in Chapter 7).

Start prioritizing your profits: When you set up your weekly schedule, make sure you start with income producing activities. Twenty percent of your activities account for 80% of your income. Figure out what those critical-inch activities are, and do more of them. Really think about the top two or three things you need to do to create more income. Now put those in your schedule consistently so you assure you are creating income. Constantly ask yourself if what you're doing is profitable, and focus on doing what you should versus what you feel. Also remember, impact drives income.

Start placing a higher value on your time: Time is more valuable than money. You can always get more money, but you can never get more time. Is it possible to become twice as valuable, and make twice as much money in the same amount of time? Of course it is. There is nothing more valuable than time invested wisely. We all have the same 24 hours. It's what you do with them that determines everything.

It's okay to say NO: This word can change your life. Is it possible you're over-extending yourself and committing to too many things? Start saying no to everything that doesn't create income for you until you get your income to a place that makes you feel confident and secure. Make a commitment to yourself that you will focus on income producing activities versus tension relieving activities. Steve Jobs even said, "It's what Apple said 'NO' to that ultimately made them successful."

Proximity is power: Most broke people hang with other broke people and they usually stay broke. Start elevating your peer group and reaching out to those playing the game of life at a higher level than you. Their belief systems, their ways of being, and their attitudes are contagious.

Lower your excuses: As the excuses go up, the bank account goes down. It's a proven fact that the best excuse makers, or who I call "validators," have the smallest bank accounts. Invest the energy and time you spend on creating excuses thinking of actual solutions that move your life forward. Excuses are a disease and those who continue making them will continue to have money issues.

Shift your focus from victim to leader: Stop blaming the economy, stop blaming your past, stop blaming your boss or company, and stop thinking the world is out to get you. Charge more for your services, switch jobs, or become more valuable.

My good friend Hal Elrod says:

> *"The moment you take responsibility for everything in your life, is the moment you can change anything in your life."*

The difference between ordinary income and extraordinary income is fast implementation. How quick will you get on your grind to start increasing your income? I assure you if you take this book seriously and want it bad enough, you will create an income explosion over the next couple of months. I want you to realize that your bank account isn't who you are; it's who you *were* before you made the decision to change it.

CHAPTER

4

THE 6 STEPS TO 6 FIGURES

"Success rewards implementation, not knowledge."

Let's talk about how this 6 Months to 6 Figure Blueprint all came about. My first entrepreneurial venture started at the age of 15 when I was introduced to eBay. Now, I didn't meet real challenge until age 20, (mainly because I wasn't going after anything challenging or worthwhile). When I got a job with a direct sales company, and became an independent sales representative. I was in charge of creating my own schedule, my own customer base, and most importantly, my own motivation. It's what I wanted and it gave me complete autonomy! I soon realized creating my own schedule and motivating myself consistently was harder than I originally thought. I really had to dedicate myself to consistent improvement, which I wasn't use to. What drew me to the opportunity was seeing 24-25 year olds who owned multiple homes and loved what they did. I wanted the same thing and knew this was the way to a great life, a life different from most.

I worked my way up to District Manager within nine months of joining the company, which was one of the quickest in the company's 60 year history. This meant I was now in charge of building my own sales organization and I could build it as big as I wanted. I underestimated the challenges of being an entrepreneur, and was quickly humbled. I realized leading and motivating others was a lot harder than motivating myself. Within a couple months, I was ready to throw in the towel and started thinking, "Maybe this entrepreneur thing isn't for me." I became depressed, miserable, and saw the money I saved disappear. The feeling of losing control over my future, letting people down, and not knowing how I was going to pay for my next meal was enough for me to make a change. I have a vivid memory of me sitting on my bed in my one-bedroom apartment, wondering what I did wrong, and why I was where I was?

I really only had two options:

Option Number 1: Abandon entrepreneurship.

Give up on the dreams, goals and ambitions I had set for myself. I could settle for an average job, but I realized if I quit, I would become accustomed to quitting and it would be easier to quit the next time something got hard.

Option Number 2: Figure it out and make it work.

I made the decision that ultimately changed my life. To never give up and figure this entrepreneur thing out. That hunger drove me to immerse myself in personal development, business, and achievement. I decided to keep working at it and make it work. I didn't want a boss and didn't want to be like the 71% who were disengaged at work, or the 69% who still have financial issues when they're 65. I heard a quote that changed my life, and I'm grateful for Joe Geneza for sharing this with me:

> *"If you want to become a millionaire, talk to billionaires - you'll get there quicker."*

I decided to ignore everybody around me who didn't have the results I was trying to achieve, and only study the best in the industry. I realized a smart person learns from their mistakes, as all successful people do, but those who operate at a world class level learn from other peoples mistakes so they can shorten their learning curve by learning from them and not wasting as much time making the same ones.

You never know how strong you are until being strong is the only option you have. I want to share my journey with you to prevent you from making the same mistakes I've made. When I began, I would have killed to have a blueprint like this, and would have avoided so much pain and struggle. I've put everything into a simple framework that I know will shift your perspective and guide you towards an amazing future. I want to share with you the exact tools and strategies I used and continue to use to create top notch results. These are transferable to *any* industry, regardless of your experience. Let's dive into these six core principles. I've made this book interactive for you and created exercises for each chapter. One of our biggest motivations as humans is the need for progress, and as Tony Robbins says,

> *"Progress is the ultimate motivation."*

Take your time with these chapters, and focus on mastery and implementation. More importantly, take consistent action and complete the exercises with focus and intention.

Here are the 6 Musts to Your First (or Next) 6 Figures:

1. *Absolute Clarity*
2. *Increasing Your Confidence Account*
3. *Shifting Your Circle of Influence*
4. *Consistent Energy and Motivation (Inner Drive)*
5. *Creating Intentional Result Rituals*

6. *Continually Focusing on Growth and Learning*

Reflecting back to the lowest points in my life, I realized I wasn't taking full responsibility for anything. I was playing the victim role, blaming the economy, my company, lack of resources, and my location. My focus was very jaded, and that's why I was where I was. I needed to change myself, my attitude, my perspective, and my intentions. The moment I got clear on that, my life shifted from complexity to simplicity. **Clarity** is the ultimate power, and if you want results you've never gotten before, you need to get crystal clear on what you want and who you are. With clarity comes motivation, but it's only when you take full responsibility for your current reality that you can change it. This was the start. Something I've learned from leadership expert Robin Sharma is to "**adopt minimalism.**" Minimalism is a great way to run your business, and a great way to run your life. Get rid of the messes and noise.

Obsession is the hallmark of genius: Don't try to be great at fifty things. Be obsessed about the few things that can really move your life and business forward.

An interesting thing happens when you start to gain clarity; your **Confidence** follows. If you don't have confidence, you will always find a way to lose. Everything you accomplish is based on the confidence you have in yourself and your ability to "make it happen." The bigger the goals, the bigger the challenges. You must realize the moment you go after your biggest goals, obstacles will show up. They are there to test your character and faith, and to see if you are serious about your goals. The person with the most confidence always wins. These days, the only security you have is the confidence in yourself and your ability to make things happen.

As John Maxwell said:

> *"It's not what you do when you're on top that makes you a great leader, it's what you do when you are on the bottom that determines your leadership ability."*

I then re-evaluated my **Circle of Influence,** because I learned that who you associate with plays a crucial roll in who you become. I didn't want to be like the people I was around. I started reaching out to those who had the success I strived for. Such a simple concept, but what a difference it made to my performance and business. There's no faster way to advance into the top 5% of your industry than this. Yet, most people don't do it. I challenge you to spend time with those people because you'll become a lot like the people you spend the most time with. Their belief systems, their ways of being, and their attitudes are contagious. Once I elevated my peer group, my standards and results followed.

I saw other entrepreneurs get pumped about new goals and achievements, and they would charge out of the gate with excitement, but they never stayed consistent. I made a commitment to consistency and that gave me a competitive edge. Lack of consistency is the subtle, but great stealer of dreams and desires. You must consistently improve your mindset, emotional intelligence, perspective, philosophy on how success is achieved, and how you view yourself. Not just when you feel like it, but consistently. This will bring the most powerful force in business, momentum, to your side. Once I saw progress and felt my mind growing, I started feeling more **Consistent Energy and Motivation.** There is nothing that brings you energy and confidence like progressing towards your goals.

When you're consistent long enough, you start figuring out what works and what doesn't, and patterns start to arise. Once I learned where my results were coming from, I **Created Result Rituals** that moved my business forward. Action was the only thing that ultimately got me out of the rut I was in, but being strategic and intentional was key. I had been working 60 - 80 hours a week, but nothing seemed to change until I figured out the result rituals that moved my business forward. Then I organized my schedule around those actions and priorities.

How do you continue to reach new heights in your life and business? **Continual Growth and Learning**, and becoming the best at what you do. This is one of the main reasons 95% of people aren't performing at a higher level. Once they reach a certain level, they stop growing. My learning didn't stop when I became successful. In fact, that's when my learning really started.

Before I go into detail on the six tactics, I want to share the most dangerous words in regards to learning and success with you. They are the words, *"I already know that,"* or, *"Yeah, I've heard that."* Those words have killed so many business goals, dreams, and income opportunities. **The questions you need to ask are:**

- Am I doing that?

- Have I mastered it?

- Does my waistline prove I have mastered that?

- Does my wallet prove I have mastered that?

- Does my business success currently prove I've mastered it?

- Do my relationships prove I have mastered that?

- Does my daily attitude and perspective prove I have mastered all of these principles?

If the answer to any of these is "no", then you have areas to improve and master. Once you become aware of what areas you want to master, you can then create an action plan that you actually do something with. Now the results can become transformational and lasting.

5

GO AGAINST THE GRAIN

*"There is NOBODY like you, and once you realize
that your entire future changes."*

Before I deep dive into the core lessons, I want to remind you how unique and different you are. In a society where everyone is trying to fit in, I challenge you to embrace being different and stand out. The story of the human race is the story of men and women selling themselves short. I'm not being negative; I'm observing the reality. The average person settles for far less than he or she is truly capable of becoming. The truth is, we're all extraordinary. We came into this world with more talents and abilities than we could ever use, but our potential is only pulled out when we're focused on our strengths, and when we stay true to who we really are. The most successful people our world has ever seen have built legacies staying true to themselves. Jody Williams, Nobel Peace Prize Winner, was asked what her key to success was and her answer was simply, "Stay true to yourself."

See? Simple, but powerful. How do you stay true to yourself

when you're surrounded by friends and/or family members who have an opinion on EVERYTHING you do, who constantly offer their opinion, whether you asked for it or not, and who seem to imply they 'know better'? It's not easy! However, if you're going to lead the life YOU really want, you're bound to run into a few people who just won't (or can't) understand where you're coming from. I'm a firm believer in mirroring the successful and doing what already works. One of the many reasons our society is struggling is people are taking advice from those who don't practice what they preach. We learn so much from what we hear so be a selective listener. One of my mentors, Isaac Tolpin, taught me this when I was 23 years old:

> *"Take very few opinions."*

That advice has served me extremely well. Start listening to voices of value, and to those who have the experience, ideas, and the reputation you're striving to emulate. Listen to people you would trade places with, and listen to people who have already experienced the success you're aiming for. Have you ever experienced or seen any of these situations? They always rub me the wrong way.

- Broke people and those in debt giving money advice.
- Those overweight giving health advice.
- Those who hate what they do giving career or business advice.
- Divorced people giving marriage advice. (Might work if they tell you what *not* to do.)
- Coaches who haven't actually gotten results giving advice on how to get results.
- Parents promoting what they learned 30 years ago, and not adapting to the new economy.
- Business professors telling students to go into debt as the first step to building a business.

I've grown up trying to fit in because I thought that's what we were supposed to do. You get reprimanded and disciplined if you speak up, act out, or try to be 'different' in school. Well, in entrepreneurship and business, it's a great way to separate yourself from the herd. When I say go against the grain, I mean stand out versus fit in, and, instead of comparing yourself to others, differentiate yourself from others. Earl Nightingale was one of the first business philosophers of our time and he said something that I'll never forget:

> *"If you really want success, and you don't have any mentors or guidance, you can get a head start by looking at what everybody else is doing and do the opposite."*

This is the foundation for how I live my life, and it should be for you, too. It is strange advice for those not familiar, but a real GAME CHANGER. It's also a great strategy for those who are serious about improving their life, business, and overall happiness. The more people do something, the less valuable it is. When I say I mirror the successful, I mean I only mirror those with the results and lifestyle I want. If you want the normal life, with normal income, normal problems, and normal experiences, this book is not for you. Let's deal in reality.

- Most people over eat and eat based on pleasure versus health.
- Most people don't have enough energy to go after their dreams and goals.
- Most people sleep in and have no morning routine.
- Most people make excuses instead of progress.
- Most people focus on the negative vs. the positive.
- Most people spend more money than they make.
- Most people talk about success vs. take action.
- Most people go to college, go into debt, and get an unrelated job afterwards.

- Most people pray for weekends and hate Mondays.

- Most people sell themselves short.

- Most people associate with people who let them off the hook versus hold them accountable.

DON'T BE LIKE MOST PEOPLE. I know deep down no one wants to be typical or average, and everyone wants to be special and different. Here's the problem: we all do the same things over and over. The majority of us live like one another and then wonder why we continually fail to achieve any real results or success in our lives. We follow each other's lead and rarely break the mold. All the greats in our society, however, live life to their own choosing, not other people's. One way to be outstanding and become more valuable is to do what others are unwilling to do. I'd rather go broke building my dreams, than just get by living somebody else's.

When I was at rock bottom and felt like I had no way out, I realized that most people would have quit, which is the exact reason I didn't. I often think, *What would the majority do?* I then continue doing the opposite because I don't want to end up like the majority. Here is an insert from the bestselling book, *The Millionaire Fast Lane,* by MJ Demarco, that explains normal perfectly:

"Normal is waking at 6 a.m., fighting traffic, and working eight hours. Normal is to slave at a job Monday through Friday, save 10%, and repeat for 50 years. Normal is to buy everything on credit. Normal is to believe the illusion that the stock market will make you rich. Normal is to believe that a faster car and a bigger house will make you happy. You're conditioned to accept normal based on society's already corrupted definition of wealth, and because of it, normal itself is corrupted. Normal is modern-day slavery. Don't be normal."

Figure out what makes you different and unique. How can you differentiate yourself from everybody else? I can assure you there is something different about you, but it's your obligation and duty to find it. One of the most important questions you can ask in business is: Why should someone do business with you versus any and every other option available to them, including doing nothing? It's time to get serious about who you are, where you want to go, and understand that an amazing life is available to you if you start thinking and acting differently than most people. I'm guessing you're reading this book because you want some or all of the following:

- **Increased income**
- **More freedom**
- **New experiences**
- **Richer lifestyle**
- **Best way to raise your family**
- **Grander view on life**

It's one thing to say you're different, but it's another to think, act, and actually live differently. Most people are struggling. MBAs are selling shoes during the day and waiting tables at night. College grads are pouring coffee and living at home until they're 29. Retirement age has morphed from 65 to six feet under, 'til death-does-employment-part.' Yet we have people who are only 19 in our Game Changers Academy who love what they do and are on track to retire by age 30. It's because they are doing things differently, and have escaped the herd. I'd strongly suggest you do the same.

6

THE POWER OF ABSOLUTE CLARITY

*"It's easy to make decisions once you determine
what your real values are."*

Ok, let's get started on the first must. Something that's evident in every achiever, every millionaire, and everybody living a world-class life is clarity. Something happens when you become clear on who you are and what you want in life. The first step for me was to get clear on what I wanted, and why. You don't need all the details, in fact you'll rarely have them at first. You just need to know what you want, and come up with enough reasons to spark some action. Action is what creates real motivation, not the other way around. For me, when I hit rock bottom, I knew two things, and that's all I needed in order to make a change.

1. I hated being broke and never wanted money problems ever again.

2. I knew I didn't want to settle for a normal job or work for somebody else.

Sometimes you must realize what's too hard for others is just right for you. Your reasons might be different, but I wouldn't read past this chapter until you gain clarity on who you are, what you want, and where you're going. There are typically only two things that motivate somebody: pain or pleasure. I was in so much pain, I decided to change and take different action. I will give you ideas and powerful questions to ask yourself to assist you in figuring out what is important to you. This is not going to be a book you read, get excited about, and then forget about two weeks later. I am serious about YOU creating your first (next) six-figure income. Most people don't know where they're going, and if you ask them what they want, they are vague and not clear enough. With fuzzy vision comes fuzzy motivation. Have you ever wondered why you're not always motivated or consistent? Part of the reason is you aren't clear on why you're doing what you're doing. If you don't know where you are going, then I can guarantee you'll end up somewhere other than where you want to be. One of our guest speakers in our Academy is Brian Tracy, and one of my favorite quotes from him is:

> *"A genius without a road map will get lost in any country, but an average person with a road map will find their way to any destination."*

In a world filled with so many options, mindless distractions, evolving technology, and information overload, it can become extremely difficult to gain clarity. Most people haven't come to grips with how important clarity is and how big a role it plays in their future. If it's unclear they are worth more than $10.00 an hour, then they will continue to work for $10.00 an hour. Clarity brings confidence and confidence raises standards.

> *"The most important thing you should protect at all times is your standards. Never let them slip."*

I'm always asking myself if my actions reflect the quality of the person I want to be and can be. If the answer is no, I ask how quickly I can adjust and adapt my actions to make sure they're congruent with my vision. Those who will see extraordinary levels of success over the next couple years understand that achieving things where you are now, giving your best now, helps the big picture of where you will be in a year or two from now. Clarity gives you power because you are coming from a place of certainty and confidence. You don't need to know your exact vision, but you have to be clear where you want to go and who you want to become. Once I committed to becoming a better leader, things became more motivating. The fears, challenges, and tough days naturally became easier. Once you become committed, your excuses will naturally lessen, and your capacity will extend naturally because you are willing to go through more.

The first thing you must do is shift from complexity to simplicity. You must get clear on your masterpiece and chip away at all the noise. Here are some very powerful questions to ask yourself before you move on.

What are the three best lessons life has taught you thus far?

1. _____

2. _____

3. _____

What are you really good at? As my good friend and extraordinary entrepreneur Honoree Corder asks, What is your area of genius? What can you become the best at in the world?

_____

_____

_____

Here's an email you can send out to the top 10 people you spend the most time with, or who know you the best to figure this out. Edit as you see fit.

Hey _____,

Thanks in advance for taking this email seriously. I genuinely appreciate your time and I know how valuable it is. I am only sending this email to the ten most influential people in my life – the people I respect most, who raise my standards, and challenge my thinking. I am reading a book about the concept of maximizing my strengths, abilities, and getting clear on what I'm best at. I really want to get outside perspectives on what others feel I am good at. I am NOT doing this at all for my ego or to fish for compliments, but simply to see how I can best serve. I want to know myself on a deeper level, and create greater clarity for my future.

I'd really appreciate your feedback of what you feel I'm good at.

It includes my talents and abilities, characteristics that describe me, what I'm good at, how I do things, what you count on me for, and any other distinguishing features you see about who I am to the core.

I would be grateful if you could respond within the next seven days if you're interested in helping me, and don't be shy about the feedback. Thanks for your support and I look forward to receiving your comments!

Thanks again,

Peter

So, it's your turn. What do others say you're really good at?

_____

_____

_____

_____

_____

Each of us has the immense potential to create amazing things in life and find lasting happiness and success, by living life on purpose. Yet, most of us barely ever scratch the surface of knowing who we truly are, let alone seeing what we have the potential to become. The purpose of your life is to discover who you are. To do this, you have to be willing to give yourself some special attention. You have to stop "going", "doing", and "chasing", and start spending more time really understanding who you are and where your creative genius lies.

One of the most defining choices you can make in your entire life is deciding what kind of person you will be on a daily basis. What will you stand for? What values, standards, and beliefs will you demonstrate each day? How do you want to live in three years, then five years? Do you want to be in a position where you don't have to worry about finances? Do you want to provide for your family? Do you want to take your kids, friends, and family out to eat whenever they want? Never miss a loved one's basketball game or your daughter's recital? These are things most people don't put a lot of thought into until it's too late.

What's important to you? In other words, what are your values? Your values make you do the things that are often not easy to do. You don't want to live life based on somebody else's values.

1. _____

2. _____

3. _____

4. _____

5. _____

<u>Examples</u>:

Flexibility

Family

Adventure

Health

Income/Financial Freedom

Impact/Influence

What would you do if you had $10 million?

_____

_____

_____

_____

_____

If you had to focus on just five goals in the next six months, what would they be? Or what five things must happen in order for you to have your best six months ever? Examples could be become #1 in your office or company, write your first book, save $10,000, double your sales, become a speaker, etc. These are called your **Big 5.**

1. _____

2. _____

3. _____

4. _____

5. _____

What are your top 3 goals for the next 90 days? These must be congruent with your Big 5.

1. _____

2. _____

3. _____

Top 3 focuses for Month 1:

1. _____

2. _____

3. _____

Top 3 focuses for Month 2:

1. _____

2. _____

3. _____

Top 3 focuses for Month 3:

1. _____

2. _____

3. _____

Remember, nothing works unless you do the work. The people who follow the strategies in this book are the ones who are going to get results, who are going to build a big business, and who are going to attract the most reps, clients, and leaders to their organization.

Now, thinking back on all the goals I've set for myself, my team, my clients, and those I have helped, there's been a common theme in all the goals that were attained. One thing was present in every single situation. The person striving for their goal had strong enough reasons to pull them through any challenge by keeping focused on the end result regardless of the circumstances.

Reasons always come first, results come second. Are you 100% clear on why you are doing what you're doing? If not, what can you do today to gain more clarity?

I would strongly recommend writing down your top twenty reasons, and then crossing out the ones that don't actually mean much, or don't spark a fire inside you. You are looking for the internal reasons, the ones that won't let you sleep in because they are so meaningful.

What are your **Top 10 most compelling reasons** to hit those goals and start elevating your life?

1. _____

2. _____

3. _____

4. _____

5. _____

6. _____

7. _____

8. _____

9. _____

10. _____

Now pick the **5** reasons that mean the most to you.

1. _____

2. _____

3. _____

4. _____

5. _____

You now know what your values are and you have your Big 5 for the next six months with your biggest reasons why. This is your mission for the next six months. You must look at these daily, write them in your planner and make them the background on your phone. This will keep you on purpose and remind you why you are working so hard. You must have goals and dreams to pull you through your toughest challenges.

Only 5% of society have their goals written on paper, and those 5% make more than the other 95% combined. When my goal was to become the quickest manager in my company's 60 year history to achieve $1 million in annual sales, I looked at my goals daily and I was constantly asking myself, am I thinking and acting like a million dollar manager? Here's the problem: people set all these big goals and want to make big money, but they aren't thinking or acting like the person they need to be to reach those goals. Now when you're reminded of your goals, you must ask yourself often, "Am I thinking and acting like the person I need to in order to achieve those goals?"

Let me demonstrate the power of asking this question. In my first full eight months as a manager in my direct sales company, our team did around $160,000. Two years later, we did over $1 million in just four months. Yes, I had more experience and a bigger team, but the main thing that changed was my thinking and how I approached each day. I was hoping to hit at least $400,000 in my first eight months, but I was thinking and acting like a $160,000 manager. I couldn't reach my $400,000 goal until I started thinking and acting like a $400,000 manager. Your results will always be congruent with who you are, how you think, and what you do on a daily basis.

Now there might be some of you who aren't excited about what you're doing right now. If what you are doing now isn't what you're called to do, or you see no chance of creating your first six-figure income there, here is what you must do. Pull out your calendar or planner and set a date six months from now to quit your job. Now you have something to look forward to and you have six months of preparation and strategizing to figure out your next move! Don't talk about doing it. Set an actual date and make it real. Hoping things will change isn't a strategy.

The Power of Reverse Engineering:

Gary Vaynerchuk engrained in my head at an early age how powerful reverse-engineering can be. He told me most don't think ahead and focus on exactly what they want. Truly productive people know the final result they are after and maintain acute clarity on what they want. Armed with this awareness, they reverse-engineer this big goal into a series of small and actionable steps that they then put into a one to two page plan of execution. This strategy works for them, and it will work for you. Take these questions seriously and focus on the ideal end results you want to create. Answer each question as if you've fast forwarded six months and created your ideal vision.

What is your ideal six month outcome?

_____

_____

_____

_____

_____

What does your business look like?

_____

_____

_____

_____

_____

What does your team look like?

_____

_____

_____

_____

_____

How involved are you in your business?

_____

_____

_____

_____

_____

How much money are you making?

Monthly? _____

Total Saved? _____

What feelings are you experiencing?

_____

_____

_____

_____

_____

If we were meeting six months from now, what would have had to happen for you to be completely satisfied with your results and progress?

_____

_____

_____

_____

_____

One of my goals with this book is to get you to THINK, and part of the reason I ask these questions is to interrupt your normal thought patterns and create new ones that are more congruent with your biggest goals. Gaining clarity is just the warm up. In order to take advantage of the goals you've identified, and create those ideal outcomes, you must improve the most important account you'll ever have.

7

YOUR MOST IMPORTANT ACCOUNT

"Insecurities will destroy you, while real confidence
will take you to a level very few attain."

Let's talk about the most important account you will ever manage. No, it's not your bank account. It's your confidence account. Everyone has something inside of them called their confidence account and everything they've accomplished up to this point has been a result of that account. I bet you can't name a visionary or exceptional leader who lacks confidence. So where does confidence come from? It comes from self-esteem and self-esteem comes from doing the things you know you should do when you know you should do them whether you feel like it or not. Scott Peck, author of *The Road Less Traveled*, says:

"Until you value yourself, you won't value your time. Until
you value your time, you won't do anything with it."

Confidence in yourself, in your abilities, and in your decision making process, is crucial for achievement. How you respond to challenges and what you believe is possible is directly correlated to your confidence account. In this 'new economy' there is NO job security anymore. The only job security you have is the confidence you have in yourself. It's your ability to figure things out and use your creative genius to seek the answers to all the problems life throws at you.

Most people are looking to outside circumstances for the answers and can't figure out why nothing is changing. You must change from the inside out and that starts with self-confidence.

Once you come from a place of confidence and develop the courage to take action on your dreams, you start to become more resourceful. The most confident leaders maximize resources and can come into the same circumstances and see opportunities where others see only problems. Here are some of the common problems and excuses facing young entrepreneurs, students, professionals, and business owners today:

"I don't have enough time."

"I don't have enough money."

"I don't have enough experience."

"I didn't get enough training."

"I don't have the right people."

"My people aren't motivated."

"I don't have the right tools or technology."

"I don't have the right plan."

"I don't like my boss."

"I don't have the right resources."

I have personally seen these excuses ruin businesses, relationships, and bank accounts. The majority of people will say they don't have the "resources." The resource belief structure keeps most people from ever leading, keeps them from earning six figures, and keeps them from building a world-class life and business. Leaders find a way to maximize whatever resources they have, as little as they may be, and they don't believe in limited resources. The ultimate resources are the feelings and emotions that make you resourceful. Tony Robbins says it perfectly:

> *"Resourcefulness the ultimate resource."*

What are the internal emotions necessary in being more resourceful?

- **Confidence**
- **Vision**
- **Creativity**
- **Courage**
- **Determination**
- **Commitment**
- **Hunger**
- **Ambition**

These are the ultimate resources. If you don't have the money, but you are creative enough, can you find the money? YES! With enough determination and commitment, you can make it work with few resources. The ultimate key is internal emotions.

What if I told you there was going to be a child who will be born in the south to a mom who is 14, and the mom will leave her shortly after? What is the future of that child? What if I told you that child will be sexually abused in her youth by family members and friends of family? By the time this child is 13, she's put into detention with other delinquents. What's the future for this child? Most people would say there is no future. What if I told you she got pregnant at 14 just like her mom, but worse, her baby was stillborn? What's the future for that child? That child was Oprah, one of the most resourceful people on the planet, and a self-made BILLIONAIRE. Oprah's a leader who has maximized her resources. Some emotion inside of her would not let her stop or settle. Now she calls all the shots.

The answers are everywhere — the internet, the library, seminars, mentorship, and even local clubs or peer groups. If you have a conversation with anybody you consider 'successful', you'll discover they have confidence above the norm - not just in themselves, but in the people who surround them. Here's the catch: they continue displaying that confidence even when nothing is going their way.

> *"If you don't have confidence you will always find a way to lose."*

Having unshakable confidence will keep you level headed when nothing is going your way. There is nothing more powerful than self-confidence in multiplying your income by two, by three, by five, and then by ten.

Here's the scary part: You're either helping or hurting your confidence at all times. There is no in-between. So everything you do, every choice you make, every person you connect with, and every action you take either gets you closer to your goals or farther away. Society doesn't think like this, and most people don't think the small choices in the moment matter. They're ALL that matter actually. Once you gain clarity on your goals, who you are, and why you're doing what you're doing, your confidence instantly increases. That's why clarity is the first must, and just by taking the action to read this book, you're building your confidence account. A lot of things can help make your confidence account stronger, and in turn, increase other important accounts including income, recognition, awards, happy relationships, progress, personal growth, etc. Before I give you my top eight strategies for increasing your confidence account, I want to introduce you to the decision train.

The Decision Train

I'm obsessed with figuring out what separates the most successful people from the majority. Most people in our society make their decisions based on their feelings. If they don't feel like working out, guess what? They don't work out. If they don't feel like waking up early, guess what? They don't wake up early. If they don't feel like getting their book done or doing their homework, they don't do it. They live their lives through feelings, emotions, and circumstances. In turn, they take a specific action —or no action— and that's their final decision. That's how they live their lives.

> *"At the end of every feeling is nothing, but at the end of every principle is a promise."*
> — Eric Thomas

Remember, if you want to be successful, look at what everybody else is doing and do the opposite. So, here's what the 5% do. These are the people who are energized, have clarity, enjoy life, are experiencing financial freedom, and are living at a level ten. They flip the script and drive the decision train in reverse. While unsuccessful people base everything off their feelings, the 5% make decisions first, regardless of how they feel. When they decide something, that's what they do, and it doesn't matter how they feel. So from their definite decision, they take action, and they feel amazing afterwards.

THE DECISION TRAIN

One of the biggest ways to build your self-esteem is to do what you say you're going to do. Every time you say you're going to do something and don't do it, your confidence decreases. Successful people make a decision, "I'm going to work out five times this week." During the week, if they don't feel like it, they pause briefly and tell themselves, "I don't care how I feel; I'm a person of my word and I commited to working out five times this week." Successful people decide what they're going to do, they take action regardless of how they feel, and as an end result, feel exceptional because they followed through on their commitment. This builds their confidence, their respect, and their incomes by making a decision and seeing it through. It is an upwards spiral from there. I've personally used this illustration for years, and it's made a massive difference in my confidence. This is a great activity to teach your sales team as well.

I'll be the first to admit, I don't always feel like doing what needs to be done, but because I know it's part of my mission and it helps people, I do it anyway.   I'm not perfect, and still base certain things on my feelings, but, it's a work in progress. When you make the decision first and follow through on that decision, you feel amazing. Doing this is not easy. If it were easy, the 95% would be doing it. You must focus on the rewards on the other side of the tough decisions. Visualize how good it's going to feel when you complete that activity you didn't feel like doing. Let's get into the eight fail-proof ways to increase your confidence.

1. Choices

If every choice you make helps or hurts your confidence, you can't be careless. The choices you make, make you. Here is one of the most powerful questions you could ask yourself when it comes to confidence:

Will this choice help or hurt my confidence?

The person with the most confidence always wins, and nobody respects an insecure leader. Successful people make choices based on who they want to become versus feeling comfortable in the moment. One of the people who made a big impact early on in my life was Isaac Tolpin, and his entire company is focused on these two words: Choose Growth. You always have two choices, the hard choice and the easy choice. When you choose growth in the moment, your confidence account builds. I want you to start making decisions based on your standards and goals, instead of on your emotions and feelings. It's tough at first, but well worth the confidence boost. Start small and continue making the tough choices until you see your confidence increase. Tony Robbins says,

"It's in the moments of decision where your destiny is shaped."

What choices can you start making today that will increase your confidence account?

_____

_____

_____

_____

_____

2. Challenges

The bigger the goals, the bigger the challenges. The moment you go after your biggest goals, obstacles will show up. They are there to test your character and faith, and to see if you are serious about your goals. Think about this: If there were no challenges, all your goals and ambitions would be easy to attain. If it didn't take much work, everybody would be doing it. It also wouldn't be worth much. If it's easy, you don't want it, and if it doesn't challenge you, it won't change you. When I was in charge of building a sales organization, I often set goals I knew I could hit. It wasn't until I started setting bigger goals that I faced real challenges. The most challenging week we ever had was also the most rewarding because of the increased results. The sales reps who broke the records went through the most challenges. My cousin, Ben, got a full ride basketball scholarship to LSU and was fortunate enough to go to the final four in 2006. One of his teammates at the time was Tyrus Thomas, who was the third pick in the 2006 NBA draft. I met Tyrus numerous times and I will never forget the tattoo he has on the back of each arm: *No Struggle, No Progress.*

Most people approach challenges with the wrong perspective and, in turn, once they find themselves in one, they let it lower their confidence. In actuality, going through a challenge should strengthen it, because you are gaining experience and a new perspective. Understanding that challenges are a good thing will not only build your confidence, but increase your awareness. It's not what you do when you're on top that makes you a great leader, it's what you do when you are on the bottom that determines your real leadership ability.

Do you really understand the importance of challenges? If you really want to strengthen your confidence account, don't wait on life to challenge you. Start challenging yourself. Like I said earlier, the only security you have is the confidence you have in yourself and your ability to *make things happen.* Job security is dead, and so is your future if you think you can find security in something besides yourself. Your adversity can be your advantage if the right perspective is adopted.

> *"The moment I used my adversity to my advantage,*
> *my career exploded."*
> — Eminem

What challenges have you gone through that have made you stronger and sharpened your perspective?

_____

_____

_____

_____

3. Consistency

Consistency is all about character. Can you do what you say you are going to do? Have you developed an identity with yourself that whatever you say your actions follow? People respect those who are consistent and stay the course regardless of what life throws at them. There have been numerous stories of athletes having an exceptional performance, but because it only happened once, their respect and credibility eventually dies down. Think about every achiever you respect. I'm guessing they've been very consistent in their life and career.

The stop-and-start process is what kills progress in any pursuit. It is probably one of the greatest reasons people don't ultimately achieve their goals and end up living lives of discontent, frustration and disappointment. Make a commitment to yourself right now that you will finish this book and use it to stay consistent throughout the year. When you stay consistent, you bring the most powerful force to your side: *momentum*. The two scariest things in life and business are:

1. Momentum

2. Lack of Momentum

In this society, consistency will give you a competitive edge and will keep momentum on your side. More importantly, consistency will continually increase your confidence.

What are 3 areas of your life that require more consistency?

1. _____

2. _____

3. _____

Why do you need to be more consistent in those areas? (Remember, reasons come first, results come second.)

_____

_____

_____

_____

_____

What would your life look like in six months if you stayed consistent?

_____

_____

_____

_____

_____

4. Repetition and Deliberate Practice

Deep daily practice is crucial to confidence. As a business person, you must practice. As a speaker, you must practice. As a sales professional, you must practice. If you work on your gifts, they will work for you. If your goal is to be a world-class leader, read everything you can on that subject. Every night before you go to sleep, watch your game tapes just like Kobe Bryant or Lebron James watch their game tapes after a game. Every single day, during your morning routine, practice. Take half an hour to write in your journal. Debrief on your day. Ask yourself questions like, how did I perform today? What can I do even better tomorrow? Practice every single day. Again, don't just go to work, but practice at getting better at what you do. Consciously challenge yourself. Come up with ways you can birth more value into the world tomorrow. Come up with ways you can be even more excellent. Like an elite athlete asks themselves how they can be more excellent at their game, ask yourself how you can be more excellent at what you do. Every single day you will get better, and eventually, you will become an expert at what you do.

5. Courage

> *"If you have big goals and dreams don't expect others to follow you, because you'll represent the strength, courage and vision they don't yet have."*

Are you doing things that scare you? Maybe this means to approach the business you are scared to talk to, or call the people you are nervous to call. Through personal experience, I've noticed that once you face your fears, they disappear. Once you act boldly, it makes it easier next time to make the tougher choice. Pretty soon, every choice you make will boost your confidence.

> *"I've missed more than 9000 shots in my career.*
> *I've lost almost 300 games. Twenty-six times,*
> *I've been trusted to take the game winning shot*
> *and missed. I've failed over and over and over*
> *again in my life. And that is why I succeed."*
> — Michael Jordan

What one action have you been putting off that would change the game for you?

_____

_____

_____

_____

_____

6. Don't Fear People

Stay fearless in everything you do. The reason most people don't take risks, live on the edge, or push the envelope is the fear of what others might think of them. If you want to live the life you truly deserve, one of significance and fulfillment, you must give up the need to be liked by everybody. Will Smith said, "Trying to get everybody to like you is the most common chosen road to mediocrity." Bill Cosby said, "You can't please everybody so don't even try. In fact, when you try, the one person you absolutely won't please is yourself." I don't know the exact key to success, but I do know the key to failure is trying to please everybody. If you can't say *no*, you will never truly be happy or accomplish the vision you have for yourself. The more you fear people, the less effective you become as a leader.

> *"People will judge you regardless,*
> *so be who you wanna be."*

7. Comparing Yourself to Others

The root of all misery is comparison, and if you're constantly comparing yourself to others you'll always be miserable. This is a very common confidence killer and will definitely diminish yours. Never let others' opinions guide your choices. Stay true to yourself by tuning out the naysayers, and instead, tune into the only opinion that really matters: your own beliefs and those who believe in and encourage you. Deep down, you know yourself better than anybody else You, and only you, are the best decision maker for your destiny. The only person you should try to be better than is the person you were yesterday.

I've been working with a young woman for the past ten months who came to me lacking clarity. She only had a couple of dollars in her bank account, lots of energy, and a desire to be the best. I rarely do one-on-one mentorship anymore, but I loved her ambition, so I decided to work with her. She wanted to be the best in her company, so she kept comparing herself to those on the company's national reports. I shared with her that becoming No. 1 by comparing herself to others is futile. "You might become number one, but it won't be as enjoyable, and you'll eventually burn yourself out. If you want to reach greatness and blow your competitors out of the water, you must focus on consistent progress and compare yourself to how you did the week before. When you make your competition the person in the mirror, you'll succeed every time." She's now the number one rep in the entire company and enjoying every step of the way. It worked for her, and it will work for you, too.

> *"Your only real competition will always*
> *be the person in the mirror."*

65

8. Confident People

Surround yourself with confident people. We'll talk more about this in the next chapter. Never forget, if you don't have confidence, you will always find a way to lose.

Understanding the importance is one thing, but implementing the steps outlined here is where the real transformation lies. Nobody is born with confidence, but anybody can improve it. So don't say you lack confidence. We all lack confidence. We all have insecurities, doubts, and fears, but the goal is to do everything we can to lower our fears and doubts while increasing our confidence and skills. You do this by choosing growth in the moment and understanding that every choice you make either helps or hurts the most important account you have. The person with the most confidence wins.

8

SHIFTING YOUR CIRCLE OF INFLUENCE

"There comes a point in your life when you realize who really matters, who never did, and who always will."

— Unknown

I remember walking down the stairs to my 450 square foot apartment late one night and thinking to myself, "I can't keep living like this. Something's gotta give." At the time, I was putting in 60-70 hours per week, but not seeing the results I wanted. I didn't understand it. I sat on my mattress, which didn't have box springs, and I started looking at my computer trying to find the answers. I was so sick of living how I was living, always worrying about money, not knowing when my next paycheck was coming, and started questioning if I was really made for success. I started asking myself what separated the most successful people from the majority who struggle? That was one of the most important questions I could have ever asked myself because it caused me to think. Suddenly, a quote I heard a couple days before popped into my head: "If you want to become a millionaire, talk to billionaires and you'll get there quicker."

Then it hit me like a ton of bricks! I needed to shift my circle of influence, and I quickly realized nobody I was communicating with was succeeding at the level I strived for. That night, I made a list of the top five people who I could reach out to in my company. My frustration and discouragement quickly turned into motivation and excitement. I realized that those who I associated with played a big role in my results, or lack thereof, up to that point. The majority of the people I was talking to and getting advice from had mediocre results. I didn't want mediocrity, and I know you don't either. It's amazing what happens mentally when you think about how much the people around you affect you.

Let's do a quick exercise. I want you add up the income of the five people you hang around with the most. Literally, estimate the income of the five people you spend the most time with. Then divide it by five. There is a good chance that your income is close to that amount. You're the average of the five people you spend the most time with. If you want to elevate your life, shift your circle of influence. Who you associate with is who you become, and who you become determines your future success.

In other words, make sure you are communicating with people who are playing the game at a higher level than you. Who is already accomplishing the success you desire? The term role model is not used enough in our society. It's extremely important to have role models. A role model will raise your standards. A role model will not let you get complacent. Finding a role model or mentor will spark your mind because they are playing the game at a higher level and will challenge you to do the same.

If you hang around five confident people, you will be the 6th.

If you hang around five intelligent people, you will be the 6th.

If you hang around five millionaires, you will be the 6th.

If you hang around five idiots, you will be the 6th.

If you hang around five broke people, you will be the 6th.

It's inevitable.

Who is currently doing what you want to be doing at the highest level? It could be the top three in your company or even your industry. Write them down.

1. _____

2. _____

3. _____

I will tell you from experience it's tougher to develop a strong mindset when you only associate with weak minded people. I would make it a priority to find a coach, mentor, or expert in your field and schedule a coffee or lunch with them. I was asked in an interview recently, "Imagine you woke up and you were 20 again. You have a laptop and only $1000. What would you do?"

What would you do?

_____

_____

_____

_____

_____

Here's what I would do: I would spend that $1000 taking successful people out to lunch in the industry that I wanted to master or become the best in. You don't know what you don't know and when you gain a fresh perspective, it gives you a sense of excitement and motivation. I had a lot of fears and false judgements about what successful people would think if I reached out to them. I didn't think I was worth their time. I assumed they were too busy, and this false belief kept me from reaching out.

Most millionaires and high performers enjoy helping young professionals and those hungry for a better life. They were once in your shoes, and they are where they are today because somebody believed in them and helped them.

The ultimate advantage in life and business is the ***Power of Anticipation***. You must be able to anticipate what's coming and what to expect. If you talk with people playing the game at a higher level than you, then they can help you see challenges and opportunities you might not be able to see. Richard Branson, Tony Robbins, Oprah Winfrey, and even Michael Jordan all admit they have mentors to challenge their thinking. The moment you stop talking to people who challenge you is the moment you are most vulnerable to complacency. Here are some disturbing, yet profound statistics:

- Each unhappy friend decreases your chances of being happy by 7%.
- Friend's marriage is ending? Your chance of divorce increases by 75%.
- Your friend is obese? You are 171% more likely to gain weight.
- Few social ties? Twice the risk of dying from heart disease.

Let me share an example of the importance of who you associate with. The strongest predictor of sales success in a study of 1000 sales personnel in a large US based international company was:

1. Their relationship skills.

2. Their social capital (who they knew).

It's very clear that the top 1% income earners have the highest social capital. The data is clear that relationships are the #1 key to your success without question. So, is building relationships with exceptional people in your weekly agenda? I'd move that to the top of the priority list.

As an entrepreneur or sales professional, building relationships is a key activity that is not only fun, but critical to your personal growth and business development. Building a successful business takes a lot of time and drive, so it's good to have a network of friends and associates to draw energy from and who keep you focused and intentional. By surrounding yourself with people who share a similar drive and ambition, you are more likely to move forward as a group. Here are six benefits of networking and shifting your circle of influence:

1. **Shared Wisdom:** Networking is great for sharing ideas and knowledge. Whether it's asking for feedback or discussing your point of view, it will help you expand your knowledge and allow you to see things from another perspective. It is also likely that within a group there will be those who have already been where you are today. This provides you with an opportunity to learn and avoid some of the common pitfalls they experienced.

2. **Opportunities:** It's natural and somewhat obvious that networking will result in opportunities. The thing you will not know is when or how they will develop. Whether it's a referral, a partnership or request for your service or product, it is important to be ready to seize opportunities when they come along. I know numerous young professionals who have gained six-figure opportunities from networking with the right people.

3. **Increased Income and Influence:** Remember you are not just gaining exposure to the people you're communicating with, but you are also building connections with their network as well. If someone they know has a need that matches your business, or if you have made a positive impression, you will likely get a referral. Networking is not just a one-way street. If someone in your network matches a business you encounter at an event, don't hesitate

to share their details. It will only strengthen your relationships.

4. **Shortened Learning Curve:** One way to learn how to do something right is to do it wrong first. Trial and error is the most common way to learn, but in order to gain the benefit, you must take action consistently. Sometimes, negative experiences turn out to be positive.

> *"I learned how to become wealthy because I asked the right questions when I was broke."*
> — Mark Cuban

You can also learn from other people's experiences, whether they are negative or positive. You can learn from both successful people and from those who have failed. Learning from the negative side of other people's experiences can be helpful. I remember seeing people around me struggle when I was coming up in the business world and I made it a point to avoid developing the same habits as them. Remember, a smart person learns from their mistakes, as all good leaders do. Those who operate at a world class level learn from other people's mistakes as well so they can shorten their learning curve and save themselves valuable time and money.

5. **Bigger (And Better) Profile:** Being visible and getting noticed is a big benefit of networking. By regularly attending business and social events, people will begin to recognize you. This can help build your reputation as a knowledgeable, reliable and supportive person when you offer useful information or tips to people who need your skills. You are also more likely to get more leads and referrals as you will be the one who pops into their mind

when they need what you offer. One of my good friends, John Ruhlin, is a great example. He's considered one of the best relationship builders on the planet. He's built great relationships with John Maxwell, Darren Hardy, over 20 sports teams, and multiple top notch CEOs. His company, The Ruhlin Group, has closed deals with some of the biggest companies in the world. I asked him what his keys were in building high level relationships and here's what he shared:

"Always give more than you think is reasonable. Most people hold back five to 10 percent because they're afraid they might be taken advantage of. They're afraid to go over the top, or set themselves apart with the fear of possibly looking foolish. Whether it's giving gifts, taking somebody out to dinner, or something as simple as opening the door, go above and beyond what others expect. This philosophy holds true to every area of your life."

6. **Lower Stress, Heightened Awareness:** By regularly networking and pushing yourself to talk to people you don't know helps increase your confidence. If you aren't uncomfortable on a daily basis, you aren't making much progress. This is an important attribute as a business owner because your business growth is dependent on talking to people and making connections. If you aren't in business yet, building relationships before you start is just as important!

We've talked about the benefits of building relationships and I hope you see the importance. Now I want to walk you through my top four strategies on developing high level relationships and how to effectively network with the most successful people on the planet. I strongly believe when you take action on these consistently, you will experience a power unlike anything else.

Elevating Your Influence

The Power of Association

Expand Your Currency

Accelerate Every Interaction

Always Be Networking

1. The Power of Association

Associations may mean being around the people who can make your success happen. Donald Trump and many other successful people do this. They associate with people they want to emulate and who can assist them in their success.

Here's a good test to determine if your associations could be sabotaging your success:

- Have you told them about your goals or desires to improve? If not, why not?

- If you have, did they laugh, downplay, or disregard your dreams, goals, and vision?

Here is what you must understand: most people do not hold us back intentionally. They aren't "bad people" who are trying to hurt us. Most people compare their success and their station in life with those around them. If someone in their circle (in this case, *you*), begins to grow and push beyond what is normal for the group, they will begin to get uncomfortable. The easiest way for them to relieve the discomfort is to keep you within the bounds of the group, so they pull you down. Have you ever experienced this? I have. If your goals, dreams, and visions of your best life are important, you have choices to make about how to deal with these people.

No one else is responsible for your success. Get your

own mind right and do all the work necessary to put yourself in the best possible position for achieving your desires. When you've reached that point and have committed to the work you must do, then you can deal with the unhealthy relationships.

The biggest thing is to handle these relationships with love. Not IN LOVE, but from a place of understanding and compassion. They aren't trying to hurt you. Anything they do to cast doubt or belittle your plans is a direct reflection of their own issues, insecurities, or regrets. Once you understand this, it becomes easier to deal with them. Talk to them about growth. Let them know how important it is to have supportive people around you and that you would like to support them as well. If they don't get on board, insulate yourself from their influence on that part of your life. How? Simply avoid sharing your goals and dreams with them.

I can't count on the fact that you're an energized type A person like me, so I'm going to point out that the best way to convince someone of the legitimacy of your goals is to accomplish them. It's really hard to argue with results. *If you walk the walk you don't need to talk the talk.* If it comes down to it and you can't escape their negativity with love, it's time to distance yourself. Sounds harsh, doesn't it? Well, it is harsh, but necessary if you want to succeed.

Trust the strength of the relationship and move on. If your relationship is strong enough, they will usually follow along once they see you are serious. Be serious. I've trained well over 4,000 people and a question I often get is, "How do I motivate others? How do I motivate my mom, sister, brother, friends, or girlfriend to dream again?" The easiest answer is to live your best life and become the best version of yourself. You can't change people, but you can point them in the right direction and lead through your lifestyle, results, and action. This is why a mentor is so important. A mentor will give you a plan and continuously push you to rise. A mentor will not allow you to get complacent. Finding a mentor will spark your mind because they're already playing the game at a higher level than you.

One of the best investments I ever made was to invest in a mentor at the end of 2008. The results of investing in myself were having my best year in 2009 and catapulting my potential. Honestly, in 2010, I didn't think I needed a mentor and did not grow at a high level, so I invested in myself again later that same year. I wanted somebody who was young, ambitious, and had a brilliant business mind, and someone who had already made their first million. I found the perfect mentor in multi-millionaire, Jordan Wirsz. The result was a record breaking year in 2011. We did more business in four months than we did in the previous 18 months. I don't say this to brag, but to show you the power in having a role model or mentor.

I would make it a priority to find a coach, mentor, or expert in the field you are in and schedule a coffee or lunch to ask them intelligent questions. You might have to pay for a mentor, and most people who can help you value their time at a high level. If you think mentorship is expensive, try mediocrity. Here's something I read in *Success Magazine,* while we're talking about investing in yourself, "Superstars focus on value, while failures focus on cost." I look back to 2008 and I invested a lot of money that year in my mentors, but the results were 10 times what they would have been if I didn't invest in myself. Remember the most powerful and useful investment you can make is in yourself. One of the world's best sales trainers and business experts, Grant Cardone, just spoke to our Game Changers. What an exceptional call and the wisdom he shared with our Young Professionals will stick with them for life. One thing he said that stood out was,

> *"More importantly than mentors is who are you staying away from."*

Evaluate Your Circle of Influence

Success Magazine asked their most successful achievers a very simple question. What's been their biggest secret to improving their results?

22% Waking Up Earlier

22% Making a Plan

16% Writing Down My Goals

3% Delegating

37% Learning From Other Achievers

This is the power of being around other achievers. The more I'm around millionaires, CEO's, ultra successful entrepreneurs, and the top 1% in different industries, I find all of them have amazing relationships. So don't forget the importance of them.

Who do you spend the most time with?

1. _____

2. _____

3. _____

4. _____

5. _____

How are those people influencing you? How are they affecting your thinking, actions, and standards?

_____

_____

_____

I learned a great activity at an event called the Experts Academy run by Brendon Burchard. He called it, "The make it or break it list." High Performers cultivate, deepen, and GENERATE new relationships with GROWTH friends. There are three types of friends: "GROWTH" friends (are very different from "OLD" friends (people you've known for a long time) or "MAINTENANCE" friends who are the people you talk with a few times a year or send Christmas cards to so you don't feel guilty.

Growth friends are the people you want to spend MORE time with because you are growing together, challenging each other, holding each other to higher standards, and making each other better. (The average American reports only having one to two best friends, and the average American also reports that they feel "lonely").

Growth Friends

Who will add value to your life? Write down your top four growth friends. Start spending more time with them!

1. _____

2. _____

3. _____

4. _____

Maintenance Friends

Write down the people who currently drag you down. Limit your time with them!

1. _____

2. _____

3. _____

4. _____

So, you should have four-to-six Growth Friends. How do you get four-to-six real growth friends?

- Make a list of your current growth friends
- Make a list of your potential growth friends (people you know but need to increase communication with)
- Schedule one 15-minute call per month with each of your potential growth friends.

Remember your "Big 5" you made for your next six months? I want you to get those out, and write them here:

1. _____

2. _____

3. _____

4. _____

5. _____

Here are some examples:

- Write or publish your book
- Generate your first six-figure income
- Start a business
- Get into grad school
- Become a paid speaker
- Invest in your first home
- Hire your first sales person
- Get to 5k in residual income
- Close $1 million in sales
- Sell 60 houses
- Get your first 100 members

These are called your focus goals, and we're going to build around those goals. Remember, **ALWAYS ASK WHO**. The key is not only what, but also who. Setting specific goals is only half the battle. When most people set goals, they fail to identify who can help them with those goals. Identifying who can help you achieve those goals is the key to attaining them.

It's extremely important you stay future-oriented. High performers are always connected to a more compelling future, whereas low performers don't maintain a vision for the future. When you reach out to those playing the game at a higher level than you, it keeps you focused on those future goals. Research has shown that multi-millionaires talk about the future nine-to-one compared to everyone else. When you hang around with people who talk about the future, you naturally talk more about the future.

When I lived in the Seattle area I met with a young entrepreneur who owned a salon. She called me and needed my help, so I did an in person one-hour session with her. These aren't cheap by the way. When somebody commits to a one-hour session, it shows they are very serious about success. She had a problem getting repeat business and wanted more customers. Don't we all? One of the things I had her do was call the top five salons in LA and ask them what they were doing to get and keep customers. What were the top 5five salons doing differently? Of course, I taught her several powerful questions to ask, told her who to speak with, and how to follow up. She reported back to me and we created a very simple, but powerful action plan. Within two months, her business doubled and she's never looked back. This is the power of learning from those who have done what you're looking to do. Learning from your own experience is the most expensive way to learn. Other people's experience is cheaper and more effective.

Your Dream Team: A good friend of mine, Jon Vroman, was speaking to our Game Changers and he brought up a brilliant idea on building your dream team. When you watch sports, you'll find the most successful teams play very well together, they compliment each other, and they all have one single focus: winning. The same goes for business and life. The people you have in your inner circle, and those you associate with the most are your team and you are the CEO. Who needs to be on your team to make sure you have a "dream team?"

2. Expand Your Currency and Add Value

When you reach out to successful people, you need to come from a place of service. How can you add value? What are you really good at? What could you contribute to them? How could you spread the word about what they do? When you do things for others before yourself and you are always looking to add value to others lives, you will naturally stand out. Most people try to turn everyone they meet into a client or prospect before ever adding value or getting to know them. That business is dead and the businesses with that attitude will fail.

The best thing you can do is invest in yourself so you have more to give. Do research, do your homework and ask how you can add value. All relationships have to start with generosity. A good networker does research on companies; a great networker does research on people. When reaching out to a high performer, you want to approach them with the mindset, "how can I add value?" I've attached an email template for you to get ideas from and use.

Subject Line: Can I promote your work?

Dear Achiever,

I respect your time at the highest level and wanted to thank you in advance for reading this! I first wanted to thank you for all you do for people, and ask if there is anything I could do to add value, promote, or spread the word about your products or programs to my circle of influence? I've been following you for quite some time now. I am/do_____. (Share what you do) I really love what you've done and I 100% believe in your cause, structure, and the legacy you're building. Is there anything specific you're doing now that you're trying to promote or something I can share?

I'm a big fan of your [insert relevant thing here: blog, book, product, event, etc.]. I particularly like your message about [insert their core message here] and it's meant a lot to me. I know it can be a thankless job being a role-model/leader, so please know your work is making a difference in people's lives. It sure has in mine.

Anyway, since we're both in the business of [insert topic here], I thought I'd share your message with my audience, even if it's not as large as yours. I help people [learn and achieve what?] so I think we have a nice alignment in how we serve.

Thanks again for all you do. Please let me know what you'd like me to tell my audience about and how I can help you. Looking forward to hearing from you!

Much Respect,

Peter

You can get a hold of anyone if you persist long enough and never give up! Rejection doesn't take anything away from you so what do you have to lose? People are a lot more willing to help than you think. When I was first starting out, I didn't know any successful people and I certainly didn't know any millionaires, so I had to learn and figure out how to get in their circles. I sent some emails asking them for an interview even though I assumed none of them would say "yes" because I didn't have a big company, website, podcast, or anything like that. To my surprise, they all said yes. Interviewing millionaires is a great way to connect with them! Even if you don't have much influence yet, this is how you begin.

3. Accelerate Every Interaction

When you actually start connecting in person with successful people, it's important you stay very open and observant to the present moment. Wherever you are, be there. How many times have you been at work wishing you were with your family and friends? Then when you get home, you think about work? I used to be at the beach wishing I could work more and then once I started working more, I would visualize being on vacation. That is a very stressful, unfulfilled way to live. I finally learned the power of being present and it transformed my relationships, lifestyle, and happiness. The most successful people live in the NOW and are focused on squeezing every last ounce out of every moment, every day, and every experience. This is a crucial part of building quality relationships and the world's best connectors always stay 100% present. When you're in a conversation, are you just waiting for the other person to stop talking so you can get your words in or are you listening with the intention to understand? The person who is most present is the most influential. Be there with them, fully engaged, fully energized, and present with piercing eye contact. Imagine there is a sign hanging from the neck of every person you connect with that reads, "The most important person in the world."

A question I ask myself often is, "What level am I at right now in my presence?" All influence comes from being present with the person in front of you.

Follow-Up: I'm sure you've heard the quote, "The fortune is in the follow up." So few people actually follow up that doing so already sets you apart from most. Can you find three ways to follow up with the person you connected with? Send them an email after meeting them expressing appreciation for them taking the time to speak with you. Better yet, send them something memorable that they won't forget. Since I used to work for a company that sold Cutco Knives, I would send the people who spent time with me some knives with their name and logo engraved on them. I've sent different knives to people like Grant Cardone, Gary Vaynerchuk, Arianna Huffington, Brian Tracy, Eric Thomas, and numerous others. It's different and unlike anything they've gotten before. Most importantly, it's memorable and this separates you from the pack.

4. Always Be Networking

You can network anywhere. Just yesterday I was in Coronado lying by the pool, and met a brilliant business man from Toronto. We spoke for about 30 minutes and I gained some great wisdom from him. Live events, seminars, and conferences are a great place to network and meet potential partners, as well as your local Starbucks. I reached out to one of my current mentors through Facebook, and he's made a profound difference in my success thus far. I can't even imagine if I hadn't had the guts to ask for five minutes of his time.

Here are a couple great networking resources for you:

- Join the Premier Community for Entrepreneurs & Professionals: www.GameChangersMovement.com.

- Business Networking International: www.BNI.com

- Entrepreneurs Organization: www.eonetwork.org

- Entrepreneur Groups: http://entrepreneur.meetup.com/

- Meet with like-minded people: www.Meetup.com

- I've met some amazing people through: www.toastmasters.org

- Young Entrepreneur Council: www.yec.co

Within the next seven days, I want you to pick one of the groups above and start networking. I can't stress enough how important it is to make sure you're communicating with those who are playing the game at a higher level than you are. Once you find the one that fits, find an accountability partner who has the same drive, ambition, and mindset you do. You can also start your own mastermind group in your area and invite those who have similar ambitions and values you do.

> *"If you're the smartest person in the room,*
> *you're in the wrong room."*
> — Richard Tirendi

Who are you going to connect with to make sure you are creating the right kind of relationships around you?

1. _____

2. _____

3. _____

4. _____

5. _____

Remember, be relentless and understand successful people appreciate persistence. Nobody fails alone and nobody succeeds alone. Always pay attention to the people around you.

"Lots of people want to ride with you in the limo, but what you want are people who will take the bus with you when the limo breaks down."

— Oprah

9

CONSISTENT ENERGY & MOTIVATION

"Those who don't make time for exercise will
eventually have to maketime for illness."

— Edward Stanley

Now that you've gained some clarity, increased your confidence account, and elevated your circle of influence, it's time to maximize your motivation and energy. What most people don't realize is that success is ongoing. It's not an event, it's not an activity that you participate in, it's not a goal, and it's not one accomplishment. It is a continuous journey. It's who you become that will determine your success, and who you become has a lot to do with your past actions. When I was broke and struggling, I didn't understand this philosophy. I was working hard and putting in the hours, but I wasn't doing anything to improve who I was becoming. A piece of advice sticks in my head from my mentor, Isaac Tolpin, "Results must be created in your business whether you feel like it or not," and he encouraged me not to leave the business until my business was able to run without me. A lot of my colleagues would work hard for a short amount of time and then take a vacation or a break, and their businesses would lose momentum. They would then have to build it back up, and that's a grueling, never ending process. They couldn't get themselves to work consistently for months at a time because it went against traditional thinking.

Creating your first six-figure income takes hard work and consistency. The year I went from broke to six figures, I missed a lot of family events, parties, movies, and didn't have the typical life a young kid in his early 20s had. Walt Disney said, "If you act like an adult when you're a kid you can afford to act like a kid the rest of your life." I want to give you the proper expectations of what success really takes. There is a lot of sacrifice and it's extremely important to keep your energy top notch when you're in the grind. Having energy gives you a competitive advantage and you want to give yourself every advantage you can. Energy also complements consistency if it's strategically used. You must focus on consistent action if you want to build real momentum. To create a six-figure income within six months, you need to create big momentum. The only way you'll experience momentum is through continuous and focused action. You must consistently improve your mindset, your emotional intelligence, perspective, and philosophy on how success is achieved and how you view yourself. Consistently - NOT when you feel like it. Once you get clear on what you want, build your confidence account, and elevate your circle of influence, you must stay consistent or you'll always be starting over.

I used to get frustrated when starting a new venture and seeing the competition leap out in front with a fast and successful start. Then I found the single discipline that gave me the advantage to beat anybody at almost anything—consistency. A lot of people get excited about new goals or new opportunities and charge out of the gate in an explosion of activity that eventually wears them out. If you make a commitment to consistency, you'll not only catch your competitors, you'll usually leave them in the dust every time. I do what I have found most people cannot—stay consistent.

Lack of consistency is the subtle, but great stealer of dreams and desires. The lack of consistency is what kills progress in many pursuits. It is probably one of the greatest reasons people don't ultimately achieve their goals and end up living lives of discontent, frustration and disappointment. In the industry of personal development, entrepreneurship, leadership, mentorship, marketing and sales, I've seen so many people wonder why they're failing to create the business or results they want. One of the most common reasons, after hundreds of conversations and taking a close look at their actions and behaviors, is they aren't consistently improving in the areas that matter most.

I was watching a documentary called *The Men Who Built America*. It portrays the lives of the most successful business moguls of ALL time - Henry Ford, JP Morgan, Andrew Carnegie and John D. Rockefeller. One of my favorite quotes from that show was from Rockefeller:

> *"If you aren't showing up to be better than you were yesterday you will not last in real business."*

On my journey towards success, I've had a chance to surround myself with great people and I've studied countless high achievers, CEO's, athletes, leaders, and brilliant entrepreneurs. Something unique was present in all of them. They had a zest for life and an amazing amount of energy. What's happening with most people is they are getting discouraged, unfocused, and letting negativity affect their attitude, while they should be putting all of their energy into finding solutions, creating better ways to move forward, and strengthening their mindset daily. In these tough economic times, it's important that you stay focused on what truly matters and avoid getting caught up in all the negativity out there. One of the biggest keys to consistency is creating consistent energy and I am going to put a lot of emphasis on this topic.

A major challenge people face right now is they don't have the energy to achieve their dreams. They are tired during the day, don't want to wake up, and feel lethargic all the time. Energy is the most underrated commodity and one of the most important factors in creating an extraordinary quality of life. Yet, in a time of constant demands, we often neglect what we know is most important. In order to take your life to the next level, it's crucial to make a commitment to living a more energized and healthy life. I know I'm dragging on about this, but I want to stress how important it really is. Nobody talks about the importance of energy in business and personal success. Without world-class levels of energy, you won't get to your best business. I've had a chance to be around numerous successful people and one of the traits of greatness is they have very high energy. Those high levels of energy get them up early in the morning without feeling exhausted during the day, allows them to work hard, and pushes them through adversity, while remaining optimistic.

I want to teach you how to create an energy explosion in your life. Think about Richard Branson, Thomas Edison, Elon Musk, Mother Teresa, and Tony Robbins. These are some of the most creative minds in the world. NONE of those people could have done what they did without high levels of energy! You can't be a leader within your community, in your company, or in your family unless you have high levels of energy.

I remember being tired all the time, dreading the mornings, and having a difficult time getting myself to work. Out of that frustration, discouragement, and lack of results became an obsession with making sure I had maximum energy and enthusiasm. I read countless books, listened to all the audios, and started working with experts, and my energy has been extraordinary ever since!

I've now put everything into a system and the system really does work. I've proven over the past few years, not just to myself, but with all those who I mentor, inspire, and influence that energy is the most important factor in creating an exceptional life. The person with the most energy in this new economy will always come out ahead. Don't take energy for granted.

What if you had the time, flexibility, and lifestyle you desire but NO energy? After all, without energy we can't perform or do anything really, even if we do buy time. If I had to pick one thing that has helped my success over the last few years it would be the level of energy I have towards my life, my career, my influence, and my family. Energy creates action and not only action, but bold action. Let's remember, energy is within us and time is outside of us. So, it makes sense to focus on energy. How do you ensure you have the energy at a level most don't? Before I dive into the framework I've created, let's go over some of my favorite benefits of staying energized:

- Increases the influence and impact you have on others
- Improves productivity and performance
- Improves relationships and higher level connections
- More passion and excitement
- Consistency and better results
- More happiness and fulfillment
- More resourceful and innovative
- More courageous and confident

Dr. Oz, who is very successful in every aspect of the word, was asked what his secret was in managing his time. He performs 250 open-heart surgeries a year, is a professor at Columbia University, a chairman of surgery, a medical program director, a prolific writer, a regular on TV and radio, including *Oprah*, and he launched his own TV show on the *Oprah Network*. Oh, and he is also a devoted husband and father of four. What he said was one of the best distinctions about time management I have ever heard: "It's not about time management. It's about energy management. That is everything."

Look for ways to get a better Return on Energy (ROE). If you are doing a good job at efficiently and effectively using your time, but you're doing things that drain your life force and steal your joy, what good are you doing? You will immediately know if you should be spending your time on something if you ask yourself whether it gives you energy or takes energy away. Spend more time on what gives you energy, and guard against, eliminate, or delegate your time for those things that deplete your energy. Make sure what gives you energy is actually congruent with your goals and dreams. If going to a movie gives you energy, that won't do much good unless it's well deserved.

If we understand that time is outside of ourselves and energy is within us, we begin to understand that energy is actually our currency for living and being. Successful people understand this at a level most don't even think about, which goes back to the choices people make.

The answer lies in the renewal of these three sources of energy:

- Physical

- Emotional

- Mental

Physical Energy

Back in 2009, one of my mentors, Jon Berghoff, said something that has stuck with me. He said, "Physical energy is 80% of your success and your energy at any given moment makes a huge difference in how well you impact others."

Let me repeat that: Physical energy is 80% of your success. Achievement is hitting a number and fulfillment is actually feeling good about it, and you can't feel good unless you have energy. Remember the question I asked you earlier? What if you had the time, flexibility, and lifestyle you desired but NO energy?

There are three parts to physical energy:

- Nutrition
- Exercise
- Sleep

Nutrition

Nutrition plays a huge role in your daily energy. Appropriate nutrition refers to managing what you put in your body, how much you eat, and realizing what foods bring you energy and what foods deplete energy. One of the easiest and best things you can do starting today is to drink lots of water. I won't go too in-depth when it comes to proper health, but I will tell you to learn what foods bring you energy and what foods to put in your body. What you put in your body affects how you look and how you feel. What you put in your head affects how you think and what you do. So watch both. Go on a ten day challenge and you'll experience an energy breakthrough like never before. Here are a couple of health tips that will make a difference for you right away:

- Try not to consume anything processed because processed foods decrease energy. Consume organic, fresh foods.

- Make sure 60-70% of your food is water-rich. Lettuce, non-starchy vegetables, fruits, and baked fish, are some examples of foods that are watery.

- Drink lots of water each day. Add lemon juice (lemon juice is acidic outside the body but is somehow alkaline inside the body). Drink water 30 minutes before and 30 minutes after each meal.

- Eat smaller portions and eat until you've had enough. Don't eat until the point of being full. The digestive process is one of the body's most energy consuming processes and when you eat more, it will take more energy away from you.

- Try not to eat past 7:30 pm. When you eat late, your body is working all night to break down the food, so you'll wake up tired.

I am not a health expert and I don't claim to have all the answers. I do want to share what I've learned, based on personal experience. Here are some foods I have found that maintain and increase my energy level:

Cucumbers, mixed greens salad, walnuts, almonds, trail mix, parsley, raw spinach, broccoli, celery, garlic, green beans, lima beans, carrots, beets, and zucchini.

You want to look for foods that are high alkaline and organic.

You can see why it is called a challenge. A lot of this seems ridiculous, and your boyfriend, girlfriend, or spouse will think you've been brainwashed. Organic and healthier food does cost more, but your body is well worth the investment. I know people don't like to spend money on something until they've tried it, but I really believe spending that money committed me to eating better. Once you feel healthy, you'll never go back. Nothing tastes as good as health feels.

What three new commitments are you going to make today regarding your nutrition?

1. _____

2. _____

3. _____

Exercise

You may be surprised to hear this, but you can't separate your body from your mind. The stronger you become physically, the stronger you become mentally. The two things I've seen disrupt businesses and delay progress are distraction and fear. Distraction and fear naturally lessen when you strengthen your body consistently. I learned, while attending Tony Robbins' Business Mastery Seminar, that fear is physical and it will lessen the more you strengthen your body. Exercise isn't just good for your outer appearance; it also affects your inner ambition.

When I say exercise, I don't mean extensive cardio. In fact, short, intense exercise is far more beneficial and achievable. Brian Tracy, Tony Robbins, Darren Hardy, Richard Branson, and Dr Oz are only a few I have studied who say they work out or do something active six to seven days a week. Work out in the morning for as little as only 15 minutes, do 20 pushups, sit ups, run, stretch, walk around the block, or go for a jog. If you keep your body healthy, your mind follows. I used to think to get a good workout in, you had to work out for at least 45 minutes. I would stress out when I couldn't get a full workout in, but realized a hard 20-minute workout is just as effective. Even 10 minutes is good to start with and is enough exercise to stimulate the receptors in your brain. Focus on progress, not perfection. Start with 10 minutes in the morning, then go to 15, and progress to 20. Go from three days a week to four days a week to five days a week.

At the start of 2012, I made a commitment to myself to work out six days a week and it's been one of the best decisions of my life. I feel better than I did when I was 18 and to experience life at a charged and energized level is priceless. I strongly recommend you do the same. Don't neglect working out and don't neglect your body because when you feel stronger physically, you feel stronger mentally. Start today! There are numerous resources online like P90x, Insanity, Jillian Michaels, and many others. Just type in "short workouts" in a search engine. These short workouts are all over, and if you want it bad enough, you'll find them.

Emotional Energy: AKA Emotional Intelligence

When it comes to happiness and success in life, emotional energy matters just as much as intellectual ability or intelligence. Emotional energy helps you build stronger relationships, succeed at work, and achieve your personal and professional goals. Emotional intelligence is a very underrated skill in the new economy, but absolutely necessary for real achievement. In order to perform at our best, we need to access our positive and uplifting emotions such as passion, ambition, determination, excitement, eagerness, and happiness.

Emotional intelligence (EQ) is the ability to identify, use, understand, and manage emotions in positive ways to relieve stress, communicate effectively, empathize with others, overcome challenges, and defuse conflict. Emotional intelligence impacts many different aspects of your daily life, such as the way you behave and the way you interact with others. If you have high emotional intelligence, you are able to recognize your own emotional state and the emotional states of others. You engage with people in a way that draws them to you. You can use this understanding of emotions to relate better to other people, form healthier relationships, achieve greater success at work, and lead a more fulfilling life.

How to Increase Your Emotional Intelligence

Write down the top five positive emotions you use the most, emotions that help you take action, deal with challenges, experience more out of life, and make you feel good in general.

Examples: Passion, Love, Courage, Excitement, Eagerness, Creativity, Intelligent, Resourceful, Focused, Motivated, Ambitious, Unstoppable, Caring, Inspired, Curious, Healthy, Alive.

1. _____

2. _____

3. _____

4. _____

5. _____

Now, write down the top five negative emotions you use the most, emotions that cause you to feel frustrated, repel people away from you and prevent you from taking action.

Examples: Hostility, Resentment, Anxiety, Distracted, Moody, Emotional, Inconsistent, Frustrated, Reactive, Intimidating, Impatient, Stubborn, Fearful, Rude, Depressed, Aggravated.

1. _____

2. _____

3. _____

4. _____

5. _____

Take a good look at those emotions you just wrote down and you'll realize something very profound. All your biggest successes, accomplishments, and best experiences have taken place operating from your positive emotions. The toughest times in your life are when you are consistently operating from your negative emotions. Most people think their way into depression. The quality of our lives is determined by the emotions we consistently display and from which we operate. When we dwell on negative emotions, the quality of our energy is hugely diminished. Over time, running on negative emotional energy at work or in any other area of life is a huge energy drain, which leads to chronic tiredness, perhaps even Chronic Fatigue Syndrome, and most importantly, lack of motivation or hunger to create a better life for yourself and others around you.

Unfortunately, part of the reason people don't pursue their dreams, or go after opportunities with confidence, is because they are tired. Are you starting to see how important energy is? This is why I dedicated an entire chapter to this subject. Please don't overlook this subject. Most people don't do much intentionally to create energy, to study energy, or to stay in their positive emotions, and so they end up tired and fatigued. Best-selling author, Mathew Kelly, said this at a recent seminar I attended:

> *"When you're tired you will make stupid decisions, and act like a coward."*
> — Matthew Kelly

The decisions you make are greatly affected by the emotional state you're in and it's our consistent decisions that shape our reality. Start to become more conscious of what state you're operating in emotionally and do everything in your power to stay in your positive emotions. I've been fortunate enough to connect with Arianna Huffington and she said something that really stood out:

> *"Never make any important decisions when you're tired, hungry, angry, or lonely."*

Just to hammer this home, I want to illustrate the importance of energy. Andrew Carnegie sold his company to JP Morgan in 1901 for $480 million, which is equivalent to $300 billion now. The book, ***Think and Grow Rich***, was actually created because of him. He was asked what he looks for in his executive board and the leaders he has under him or hires. He said he only looks for two things:

- Ability to energize themselves

- Ability to energize others

Are you starting to understand how important energy and enthusiasm are in life and business?

What three new commitments are you going to make today regarding your Emotional Energy?

1. _____

2. _____

3. _____

<u>**Mental Energy**</u>

Mental strength is a very important component to real achievement. Renewing our mental energy makes us far more intelligent and productive in the long run. To perform at our best, we also need to sustain concentration and be flexible in our thinking with appropriate focus and concentration. Be careful what you let enter your mind daily because what you think about starts everything. You will always act based on what thoughts come first. Our mind is always being fed. It's important to stand guard to the door of your mind and be very selective with what information you collect.

All problems are created by the undisciplined mind. The mind that isn't fed intelligence is usually fed useless information. Your mind becomes disciplined or weaker by what you feed it every day. What you put in your mind should be congruent with your future vision if you want to turn aspirations into reality.

We only have one mind and how you treat your mind is crucial to your current success and creating the future you envision. So how do you spark your mind daily? You're already so busy with school, your business, kids, sports, and all of your daily tasks. The best time to do this is in the morning. Exercising this discipline first thing in the morning is the most intelligent use of this activity. Most successful people I have studied and communicated with, including me, do mental exercise first thing in the morning.

When I was working 65-80 hours per week, I felt like I didn't have time for anything and I still wasn't getting the results I wanted! Something had to change, and it was my approach to my day. I started waking up at 5 a.m., and sparking my mind, writing my goals down, and working out. Within a couple of weeks, I felt my energy, productivity, and mindset increase. Something that can improve your mental mindset immediately is a solid morning routine. I call it your prize fighter routine, which I stole from Robin Sharma.

Crafting a Morning Routine

I always look to find the outcome in everything I do. People who are outcome related produce results like nobody else. When you think strategically and understand the purpose of the activities you're doing, it's easier to sell yourself to them. I believe there are two main reasons you need a morning routine:

1. To give you more confidence, courage, and conviction at the start of your day.

2. To figure out your most important priorities so you're more intentional throughout your day. Remember, a huge key to productivity is deciding what you're going to work on other than in the moment, and then practicing that high value work over and over until it's natural, habitual and automatic.

Never start your day without writing it on paper first. Don't leave your life up to feelings, circumstances, or chance. A life best lived is a life lived by design. Write down your most important priorities, rituals of success, and time to reflect, then ruthlessly hold yourself accountable to your schedule. Either you run your day or your day runs you. After a couple months of your days running you, you're at the mercy of your business. I would highly recommend the book, *The Miracle Morning*, by my good friend, Hal Elrod, if you want to dive deeper into your morning routine. It's really a game changer.

You must focus at the start of each day on getting into a highly resourceful mental state because when you are in a more resourceful state, you think, act and feel better. This in turn will help you make better decisions, and, of course, more productive ones as well.

The worst thing you can do is get up and go. That's how you'll guarantee an unproductive day. You're more susceptible to just react to whatever happens that day versus being in full control. The first thing most people do to start their day is press the snooze button. When you start your day resisting life, it's very challenging to create an amazing day. Think about that.

Here are some ideas that you can start implementing right away:

Read a Good Book for 30 Minutes: Books, autobiographies, magazines like *Forbes, Success, Entrepreneur*, or anything that sparks your mind positively, ignite your endorphins and allow your brain to be more alert.

Journal: You can write about what you're learning, what you're excited about, or the biggest lessons you've learned. Get everything out of your mind onto paper. You want to start your day fresh, and when you get your thoughts onto paper, you can then organize them. I ask myself these three questions every morning before I start my day:

- What am I excited about?

- What am I grateful for today?

- What am I committed to make happen today?

Success Audio or Video: A simple audio or video can

jumpstart your day. YouTube is a great resource. A lot of people are listening to our Young Entreprenuer Lifestyle Podcast in the morning. You can learn more at www.YoungEntrepreneur Lifestyle.com/itunes. They are very short, but powerful, and will shift your thinking before you begin your day. Doing this in the morning is powerful as it gives you confidence instead of fear because you are getting perspective instead of getting stressed. You start thinking about your goals, values, and the best opportunities in your business rather than randomly or mindlessly going about your day.

Spark Your Body: We talked about it earlier in this chapter, but do something active. You can feel the effects of a workout up to 12 hours after, and this also helps you stay focused throughout the day.

MVPs: Write down your *Most Valuable Priorities.* Organize and prioritize your schedule based on your vision and goals.

Visualize: For this to be effective, you must visualize with precision and detail. Peak Performers mentally rehearse their desired future daily and continue doing so until they've accomplished their goals. I want to share an excerpt from my good friend, Hal Elrod's book, *The Miracle Morning*:

"You close your eyes, or you look at your vision board, and you visualize. Your visualization could include your goals, what it will look and feel like when you reach them. You could visualize the day going perfectly, see yourself enjoying your work, smiling and laughing with your family, or your significant other, and easily accomplishing all that you intend to accomplish for that day. You see what it will look like, you feel what it will feel like, and you experience the joy of what you will create."

Write Down Your Goals: You now have a list of your Big 5 goals for the next 12 months. Looking at them daily keeps you focused on your purpose and reminds you why you are working so hard. You must have goals and dreams to pull you through your toughest challenges. Only 5% of society have their goals written on paper, and those 5% make more than the other 95% combined.

Focus on Gratitude No matter what the circumstances are, no matter what cards life deals you, there is always something worthy of gratitude. Focus on filling your mind with gratitude. All successful people practice being grateful. The best entrepreneurs, parents, athletes, and sales professionals have a gratitude practice. While most are worried about economic crisis and turmoil, the best ones ask:

- What am I grateful for?

- What are my opportunities?

- What's good about this crisis?

How can I improve my situation and use these tough times to inspire others?

Stay focused on the good things versus focusing on negativity and you will feel your motivation, happiness, and energy increase. Also, you are filling your mind with gratitude instead of the news or radio, which are mostly negative. All millionaires practice gratitude.

I've seen first-hand how much of an effect a morning routine can have on somebody's life, business, goals, and overall motivation. How you start your day determines the effectiveness of the entire day and when you take care of your days, the weeks take care of themselves. Here are a few more ideas for improving your mental energy:

Keep A Good Circle Of Friends: The greatest support system in the world is good friends. You can't be careless here. You need quality friends. Friends are those people who know all about you and still like you. Take care of them and they will take care of you. Inspire them and they will inspire you. Nothing is more valuable than your inner circle and the greatest gift is one person caring for another.

Stay Away from Toxic People: This is one of the greatest ways to increase your peace of mind, energy, and motivation. Say goodbye to the people who suck your energy The people around you should energize you versus deplete your energy. Make sure you're around people who challenge you and hold you accountable versus letting you off the hook. Your standards will rise and fall based on who you associate with. You won't believe how much stress is released once you decide to minimize your time with those who complain, play the role of victim, or make excuses.

Powerful Questions:

A solid morning routine is a CRUCIAL part of maximizing your day. What's your current routine? If you don't have one, create a morning routine right now. I call my morning routine my prize fighter routine.

1. _____

2. _____

3. _____

4. _____

5. _____

How are you showing up every day?

_____

_____

_____

_____

_____

How must you show up every day if you want to make your dreams, vision, and goals a reality?

_____

_____

_____

_____

_____

10

PEAK PERFORMANCE
SECRETS OF THE WORLD'S GREATEST

*"I demand more from myself than anybody
else could possibly expect of me."*

— Julius Erving

Before I get into the next must, I want to expand on peak performance and achievement. What makes an *Elite Performer* isn't how they show up when everything is going well. It's the way they deliver when their best laid plans are falling apart. Peak productivity is not about luck. It's about dedication and awareness. Regardless of your current situation, what business you're in, or what your goals are, this chapter is extremely important. It's your job to figure out how to work at your personal best. In a time of constant movement, constant communication, and continual achievement, the long list of to-dos and completed tasks at the end of the day makes us feel like we will never get ahead. It seems like our days are controlling us versus us taking control of our days.

This behavior of constant busyness and lack of rituals can actually take you off course from your high-value goals, hurt your physical, psychological and emotional systems, and can even damage or destroy relationships.

Before I get into my specific productivity practices, let me give you some 'Perspective Changers.' Changing your perspective can change your life. Tim Ferris has an amazing book called, *The Four Hour Workweek*, and a lot of these ideas I share here I originally learned from his book. I've experimented with all of these and have implemented them into my life and business over the past two years. I am only including those ideas that I have seen increase my productivity and results.

80/20 Everything

This is called Pareto's Law and can be summarized as follows: 80% of the outputs result from 20% of the inputs. If you take 10 of your tasks and activities you want to get done, two of them will produce more results than the other eight combined. This is a proven fact. Sometimes, when we get busy, we feel we must get a ton of tasks done versus the few important ones that create the greatest results. I'm often challenged to think intelligently about which 20% of my tasks to do with absolute focus that will YIELD huge results. This perspective flip was a big part of increasing business, while decreasing my hours. Remember, it's not the hours you work, but the work you put into those hours.

Which 20% of your tasks are resulting in 80% of your desired outcomes and happiness?

_____

_____

_____

_____

Which 20% of your tasks are causing 80% of your problems and unhappiness?

_____

_____

_____

_____

_____

_____

Most Things Don't Matter

Most things make no difference and aren't moving your life or business forward. In fact, most of the things you do in your business don't accelerate growth—they just 'maintain' at best. Being busy is a form of laziness - lazy thinking and indiscriminate action. Being overwhelmed is often as unproductive as doing nothing and is far more unpleasant. Being selective and taking more intelligent action is the path to being highly productive. Focus on the important few and ignore or delegate the rest. At the beginning of my journey towards success, I thought I had to do everything myself and didn't realize most activities didn't actually increase my business results. If somebody can perform tasks almost as well as you, delegate those tasks and stick to what you do best. Your time is more valuable doing the things no one else can do.

What activities can you either delegate or stop doing right now?

_____

_____

_____

_____

_____

_____

This is called the List to Freedom and can save you years of headache and frustration:

- *Don't like doing* - Figure out the things you don't like doing and either delegate, delete, or pay somebody else to do them.
- *Can't do* - Find other people who are the best at what you can't do. Everybody has specific strengths.
- *Shouldn't be doing* - If your time is worth $50 an hour, you shouldn't be doing anything less than that.

Don't Do Unimportant Things Well

Doing something unimportant well doesn't make it any more important. Activities that are not connected to an outcome or purpose are the drain of all fortune. Understand what you do is a lot more important than how you do it. Effectiveness is still important, but it is useless unless applied to the right things. There are a handful of things you could be focusing on that will create exceptional outcomes for your goals. It's easy to get caught in a flood of trivial matters, and the key to not feeling rushed is remembering that lack of time is actually lack of priorities. Take time to stop and re-focus your priorities as often as needed. Intelligent thinking combined with the right action will get your productivity to a level few attain. Remember what Jim Collins said in his best-seller, *Good To Great,*

> "If you have more than three priorities,
> you don't have any."

Parkinson's Law

Parkinson's Law dictates that a task will become bigger in importance and complexity in relation to the time allotted for its completion. I have personally found magic and high value in deadlines. If I give you 12 hours to complete a project, the time pressure forces you to focus on execution, and you have no choice but to do only the essentials that actually matter. If I give you a week to complete the same task, then you have six days of validation, excuses, and procrastination and one day of rushed work. If I give you a month, it becomes a mental monster. The end results of deadlines are always of equal or higher quality due to greater, more intense focus. Once you determine your result rituals, place time limits on each so you have urgency. We'll get to the result rituals in the next chapter.

Identify the few critical tasks that contribute most to your business results and schedule them with very clear deadlines. If you haven't identified your critical tasks and set aggressive start and end times for them, the unimportant becomes the important. Even if you know what's critical, without deadlines that create focus, the minor tasks forced upon you will consume time until another minuscule task jumps in to replace it, leaving you at the end of the day with nothing accomplished. I spent months jumping from one interruption to the next, feeling run by my business instead of the other way around. Don't make the same mistake. Adopt result rituals into your daily agenda today.

Here are my Top 10 Game Changing Productivity Strategies for you to implement, study, and teach to those you lead. Don't try to put these into practice all at once. Rather, pick and choose the ones you feel would make the biggest difference in your business. Once you see results and they're engrained in your day to day business, then move on to the next one. Remember, mastery versus overload. Some of these will be review, but repetition is the father of learning.

MY TOP 10 GAME CHANGING PRODUCTIVITY STRATEGIES

- **Refuse Interference:** I fiercely fight distraction in my own life and teach the teams I work with the same. Everyone's fighting for your focus. Too many people are stealing your attention. Don't be so generous in giving it to them—unless it's for something that truly matters to you. So, clean out the distractions in your workspace and personal life. I learned from Robin Sharma that Special Forces on a military mission are kept in isolation from other teams and denied access to TV/Newspapers/Internet. Why? To PROTECT their focus so they deliver perfection on their goals. So please remember: Distraction is the greatest thief of time, and time is a non-renewable resource.

- **Stop Multi-Tasking:** The larger point here is that so few of us are fully present to the work/activity in front of us. I see people with their spouse at dinner checking their Twitter feed. I see front desk employees at hotels reviewing their emails and text messaging their friends. I see people who paid thousands of dollars to be at a seminar in the back of the room playing games online instead of participating. A huge competitive advantage falls to the one in 100 performer with the brilliance to develop the skill of becoming massively focused on the one thing in front of them—truly a *Game-Changing* move.

- **Make Decisions Based on Standards, Not Emotions:** I strongly challenge you to start basing your decisions on your standards and goals rather than your current emotions. One of my mentors, Jordan Wirsz, taught me the importance of emotional IQ and ingrained this in my head: "The decisions you make based off emotion are usually the wrong decisions." I've used that advice ever since and I've seen my influence, income, and results skyrocket as a result.

- **Kill Procrastination:** So many of us procrastinate by waiting for ideal conditions to get big things done. Stop waiting for perfect conditions or the perfect product before you get to the market or take action. You want experiments, not perfection. Yes, I stand for ensuring anything you offer is the best it can be, but sometimes putting off a project until it's flawless demonstrates your fear of failure. And we both know you're a lot bigger than that.

- **Write a Stop Doing List:** Stop living week by week. A stop doing list is sometimes more important than a to-do list. Every productive person obsessively sets to-do lists. But those who play at a world-class level also record what they commit to stop doing. Steve Jobs said what made Apple successful was not so much what they chose to build, but all the projects they chose to ignore. Make a stop doing list today.

- **Get In The Zone:** We're ADDICTED to distractions. Most people get distracted because distraction is physically addictive! Our brains love distraction. Every time you get distracted, your brain releases dopamine (the 'feel good' drug). So, when you see you have a new email, or a new text message on your phone, or you get a notification from Words with Friends, letting you know it's your turn, you drop everything to get your 'dopamine fix.' You are three times more productive when you're in the zone, and you only get in the zone when you zero in and concentrate. Don't be so available to everyone. I often spend hours at a time in a coffee shop or hotel lobby. I turn off my devices and think, create, plan and write. Zero interruptions. Pure focus. Massive results. You can get more done in 20 minutes of focus than three hours of distraction. Remember, focus is more important than intelligence.

- **Sell Yourself:** The reason why most people can't focus consistently is because they haven't actually sold themselves on the task at hand or the goal they are trying to accomplish. By sold, I mean they have cut out the alternative. They know the importance of what they are doing and the purpose and ideal outcome they are seeking to attain. If you procrastinate, then you haven't sold yourself on your goal or task yet. Don't get yourself involved unless you are sold on the activity and its purpose in moving you forward. If you're not sold on your significant other, then there is a good chance you'll break up. If you haven't sold yourself on how bad smoking is, then you'll keep smoking. What do you need to sell yourself on?

- **Show Up Charged:** How you show up is exactly how your entire day unfolds. Show up with energy and strength and you will be more productive. A morning routine is crucial to creating a productive day. All the successful people I have ever met, studied, or read about, start their morning in a very powerful way. Do your actions and thoughts in the morning set you up for a winning day, or 'just another day?' The goal is to get as much from the day as you can and not just to get through the day.

- **Get Great at Reverse Engineering:** Here's another lesson learned from Gary Vaynerchuk and Robin Sharma. Engineers working with technology startups are masterful at taking a competitor's product and breaking it apart – piece by piece – from the finished version to its initial components. After studying the pieces, they then make their own product even better. Truly productive people do the same thing with their most valuable opportunity. They know the final result they are after and maintain acute clarity until they reach the desired result. Armed with this awareness, they reverse engineer this big goal into a series of small and actionable steps that they can then put into a one to two page plan of execution. This strategy works for them, and it'll work for you.

- **Practice Productivity:** The more you PRACTICE what you know, the better you get. There's the state of passively knowing something and then there's the level of performance you attain when you consistently PRACTICE what you know. Professional basketball players know how to shoot a free-throw, but they still shoot them every day, over and over again, because they are committed to reaching a higher level of performance. Practice what you know over and over again because this is going to build your muscle memory, meaning if you practiced the technique relentlessly, a time will come when you perform it swiftly, elegantly and unconsciously. The same applies to your productivity. Practice doing work that matters. Practice sitting in one place for many hours focused on a single result. Practice running rituals and elite performance routines that will lift you up into the realm of world-class. Because, as I know you know, genius isn't so much about genetics as it is about work ethics and sheer practice.

I strongly recommend examining your own life and incorporating these principles into your daily routine on your journey to your extreme achievement. These steps, if applied, will help you transform your productivity, performance, and lifestyle. This is just the beginning. Remember: It's not what you know; it's what you do with what you know. The actions you take with regard to this information is where the real power of change and transformation reside. Now let's dive deep into creating customized rituals for you.

11

CRAFTING THE PERFECT RESULTS RITUALS

"The amount of stress you have in your life is in direct correlation to the lack of rituals you have in place!"

— Davey Tyburski

We've talked about gaining clarity, developing a confidence account, shifting your circle of influence, and making sure you're consistent with your energy and motivation. These are crucial for extreme achievement, but without the right rituals and habits, your long term growth will be stunted. Let's continue to build your success system and make sure it's sustainable over the long term. I know a lot of business owners and entrepreneurs who got into business to be in control and build a great lifestyle, but they ended up being a slave to their businesses. That's what we're trying to avoid. Once I finally hit our sales goal of over $1 million for the year, I wasn't satisfied because I was working over 80 hours a week. I wanted the results and the lifestyle. Of course, those who haven't created both will tell you it's impossible. Never let those who have given up on their dreams talk you out of yours. I've seen numerous people get talked out of pursuing their true potential by those who placed their own limiting beliefs on others. In order to experience consistent business growth while building a great lifestyle, you need result rituals in place.

A ritual is something you do consistently that has a proven track record of getting results. Some call them routines, some call them systems, but they mean the same thing. Once they're in place, they require little or no attention from you. Result rituals deliver predictable and consistent results. Always strive to put systems in place because the right systems can transform your life and business. As I watched and studied the most successful people, I realized something that I hadn't noticed before. They create routines for everything they do and are also strategic in which rituals they implement in their lives. They don't leave their success up to how they feel, luck, or other people. They assure their success and guarantee their progress by having routines for the most important aspects of their lives and businesses. If you look at the most productive people on Earth, people like Stephen King, Tony Robbins, Richard Branson, Michael Jordan, Dr. Oz, and Oprah, you'll discover that they all follow strict daily routines. (I.e., when they get up, when they start work, what they do consistently, when they exercise and when they relax.)

They surely don't leave their productivity to the fleeting winds of inspiration. Instead, they incorporate precise rituals into their daily lives that allow their creativity to flourish. Stephen King, for example, sits down to work at 8 am every morning, in the same chair, with his papers set in the same way because he knows,

> *"Obsessive consistency sends a signal to my mind to focus and deliver serious results."*

Dan Kennedy, who is one of the best marketers of all time, says, "I don't just write when I feel like writing, I write every day. I write uninspired, unmotivated, when I don't feel like it, on airplanes, in hotel rooms, and everywhere I can." Motivation doesn't create action. Actually, it's the other way around. Action is what produces the motivation to continue taking action. Many people think they need motivation to take action, but that is totally backwards.

99% of everything we do each day is habitual. When you develop a habit of doing what you should versus what you feel, the habit becomes easier over time. Most people are thinking the same thing they thought about yesterday and rarely ever have original thoughts. They do the same things they did last week and rarely focus on improving their habits. Successful people understand that their habits are either elevating them to new levels of success or hindering their progress, which is exactly why they are so intentional with what they do on a daily basis. I want to share a powerful poem with you to illustrate the importance of this subject.

I am your constant companion.

I am your greatest helper or your heaviest burden.
I will push you onward or drag you down to failure.

I am completely at your command.

Half the things you do, you might just
as well turn over to me, and I will be able to do them
quickly and correctly.

I am easily managed; you must merely be firm with me.

Show me exactly how you want something done,
and after a few lessons I will do it automatically.

I am the servant of all great men, and, alas,
of all failures as well.

Those who are great, I have made great.

Those who are failures, I have made failures.

I am not a machine, though I work with all the precision
of a machine, plus, the intelligence of a man.

You may run me for profit, or run me for ruin; it makes
no difference to me. Take me, train me, be firm with me
and I will put the world at your feet.

Be easy with me, and I will destroy you.

Who am I?

I am a HABIT!

"Be easy with me and I'll destroy you." If you don't take full control over your habits and strategically develop them, you'll be in for a rough ride. I first heard that poem years ago, and it has stayed with me ever since. When was the last time you took time to reflect on your habits? I realized, through training, consulting, mentoring, and observing thousands of young entrepreneurs, that the best way to predict somebody's next six months of results was to look at their past six months. You'll hear people talk about improving and they will swear they are going to elevate their game, but when the results are tracked, they are doing the same thing. Why? Habits define you, and if you don't make a definite decision to break habits and replace them with more intelligent ones, it's nearly impossible to change.

Habits will always trump inspiration. Inspiration is needed to create consistent action, but your habits are ultimately going to define your success or failure. It's been said that after seminars and conferences, only 5% actually use what they've learned. Why is that? It's because inspiration is very short-term and feels good in the moment but doesn't last past the activity producing the inspiration. In our Game Changers Academy, we focus on shifting habits, gaining better perspective, and interrupting bad thought patterns instead of simply focusing on inspiration or what makes us feel good. I've realized that the biggest inspiration of all is seeing progress and results, which comes from daily habits. When you begin the formation of a new habit, stick to it, and see the lasting change in your new-found life!

Do you have routines that ensure you're improving your habits, making progress, and getting results? How do you decide what to create rituals for? It depends on what you want to improve, systemize, and focus on in your life. You can create rituals for just about anything, including productivity, income, health, personal growth, innovation, mindset, adventure, increased energy, etc. Creating routines that happen every week regardless of how you feel or your emotions is crucial for sustained progress. I am going to share a couple of crucial rituals I've developed. These specific rituals have helped me create my current lifestyle. Remember, you can create rituals for anything. The more rituals you put in place, the less stress you'll experience, and the more successful you'll be.

I realized that the top 1% protect their mind and continue to improve their mental toughness so I created rituals to keep my mindset top notch. Health is an extremely important part of success and once I realized my energy was a huge part of my productivity, I created rituals that supported increased energy. You've already defined your Big 5 goals for the next six months, now it's time for you to build the key habits you need to turn those goals into rituals and routines. I am including some of mine as examples. Yours are going to be different, but I wanted to show you what rituals look like so you can create rituals that are best for you.

Mindset Rituals:

- Talk to a mentor/somebody playing the game at a higher level than me twice a week.

- Don't listen to or watch the news — ever.

- Read 20 pages per day. Make sure it's something that is congruent with my monthly and yearly goals.

- Mon-Thurs listen to personal growth/business audios in car.

- Pause and reflect weekly.

Health Rituals:

- Eat foods to elevate energy and health rather than for taste and pleasure.

- Workout 6 days per week. (Short, powerful workouts.)

- Drink a lot of water throughout the day.

- 60% - 70% greens with every meal.

- Don't eat past 7:30 p.m.

Productivity Rituals:

- Always have clarity and look at my goals daily.

- Execute my early morning routine consistently (5 - 6 a.m.).

- Complete my weekly master plan EVERY Sunday.

- 5 x 5 Rule - Look at my goals for five minutes in the morning and for five minutes in the evening..

Always ask myself these 3 questions in the morning:

- What am I grateful for?

- What am I excited about today?

- What am I 100% dedicated to making happen this week?

Once again, my rituals aren't right or wrong. They are based on my goals and vision. You must identify what's important to you and make sure your rituals are congruent with your big picture.

Here are two more powerful questions I ask myself at the beginning of each month: What are the rituals and routines I'm committed to that aren't negotiable? What MUST HAPPEN to continue creating results in my life and business regardless of whether I'm there or not?

What are my 'Non - Negotiables?'

- Always have 100% clarity on what I'm doing and why

- Add consistent value to the marketplace.

- Working out at least five times per week.

- Reaching out weekly to those playing the game at a higher

level than I am.

- Never have a job and always do what I choose. No restrictions and 100% autonomy.

- Be present, and treat every person I meet like the most important person in the world.

- Stay grateful and focused on my most important priorities.

What three result rituals do you need to stay focused?

1. _____

2. _____

3. _____

Write your rituals below and write down the five actions you are going to take to ensure you follow through.

Ritual 1:

1. _____

2. _____

3. _____

4. _____

5. _____

Ritual 2:

1. _____

2. _____

3. _____

4. _____

5. _____

Ritual 3:

1. _____

2. _____

3. _____

4. _____

5. _____

Do you see the power of result rituals? If you aren't sold on creating rituals, please read this chapter again because I know firsthand how important result rituals are for peace of mind, productivity, and business.

CHAPTER

12

CONTINUAL GROWTH & LEARNING

"Stay humble, but never lose your hunger."

The information laid out in the first 11 chapters will set you up for massive success, catapult you towards your first six-figure income, and give you the competitive advantage over those around you. To sustain that success month after month and year after year, you need continual growth and learning. Strategically designing a world class life isn't what most think about, especially at a young age. Anybody can become successful for a short amount of time, but to continue producing results above the norm is where most people fall short. Learning, studying, and investing in yourself doesn't stop when you become successful. That's only the beginning.

Over the last fews years, I've purposely surrounded myself with top notch entrepreneurs, millionaires, CEOs, and visionaries because I wanted to see how they've stayed successful and sustained consistent growth. I realized it wasn't where they grew up or how intelligent they were. Nor was it from inheriting wealth or from simply working hard. The 5% are relentless students who learn, study, and invest in themselves constantly. Kevin Eastman, Vice President of Basketball Operations for the LA Clippers, told me he reads for two hours every day. Here's the amazing part: he hasn't missed a day in 15 years. How serious are you about learning? Investing in mentors, mastermind groups, seminars, books, and audios is a regular part of their lifestyle. It's what keeps them inspired, fresh, enthusiastic, and vibrant.

I wish I would have gotten this concept earlier in my career. I certainly would have advanced quicker. I only understood it when Dan Casetta, someone I admired in my previous company, shared what he heard originally from Jim Rohn:

> *"Your level of success will seldom exceed your level of personal development."*

At that moment, I knew I needed to grow more because I realized that everybody I admired and wanted to be like was consistently reading and investing in themselves. I made a commitment to grow consistently, NOT just when I felt like it. The 5% realize they must grow into their goals before they can accomplish them. If you want to have more, you must become more.

> *"Success is something you attract by the person you become."*
> — Jim Rohn

Your education doesn't end at graduation. The sooner you understand that all of the skills you need to learn to succeed will occur after you leave the confines of the educational system, the sooner you will succeed. If you are in school, make sure you know exactly why you're there and how it will benefit your future. Don't guess or hope, but strategically think about why you're doing what you're doing.

We've covered a lot in this book and more importantly, we've created action plans for your most important goals. Don't stop there. You have to continue to improve day after day. Success isn't a sometimes thing. Success is a daily thing. When I first heard the concept of personal development, I was overwhelmed and didn't know where to start. Just start. That's the key.

> *"An ounce of action is worth a ton of theory."*
> — Ralph Waldo Emerson

While attending Tony Robbins' Business Mastery event, I learned something that I'll never forget. Don't get me wrong. I learned a lot of useful information, but this stood out more than anything else. He was talking about the most successful people he'd ever met and what they all had in common. These are people like Richard Branson, Oprah, Dr. Oz, Steve Wynn, Mark Cuban, and Donna Karen. From the world's most successful business moguls to super star athletes, he realized there were three things they did consistently that the 99% didn't do. These are the choices they have chosen consistently to create the string of success they are currently experiencing, as well as their past accomplishments. I have talked about these briefly, but implementation of all three is where the transformation lies. I am purposely repeating certain philosophies and tactics in this book for the simple reason that repetition is the key to learning.

1. They protect and spark their mind daily.

These people are extremely protective over their conscious and subconscious minds and do everything they can to keep their mindset top notch. Be careful what you let enter your mind daily because what you think is what comes about. You will always act based on what thoughts come first and the scary thing is our minds are always being bombarded with thoughts. It's up to you to stand guard to the door of your mind and that's exactly what the top achievers do. Avoid filling your mind with useless information. Your mind either becomes disciplined or weaker by what you decide to let in every day.

You only have one mind and how you treat your mind is crucial to your current success and creating the future you envision. You might ask, "Peter, how to do I spark my mind daily or when do I do that because I'm already so busy with school, my business, kids, sports, and all of my daily tasks?" Refer back to chapter 10 to learn how to become more productive. Exercising this discipline first thing in the morning is the most intelligent use of your time. Below are some suggestions you can start using right now:

Read a Good Book for 30 Minutes a Day: Start with 10 pages a day and increase consistently. If Kevin Eastman can run an NBA team, take care of his family, and read two hours a day for the past 15 years, you can do it for at least 30 minutes.

Journal Daily: You can journal about anything you'd like. What you are learning, what you are excited about, and what your perfect day would look like. Let me remind you of the three questions I ask myself every morning:

- What am I excited about?

- What am I grateful for today?

- What am I committed to make happen today, no matter what?

Success Audio or Video: As Brian Tracy says, you can turn your vehicle into a mobile university. Audio learning has been described as "the most important advance in education since the invention of the printing press." According to the University of Southern California, you can get the equivalent of a full-time university degree by listening to educational audio programs as you drive from place to place. Turn your car into a "university on wheels."

When we were teenagers, we got into the habit of driving around with our friends and listening to music. We formed the association that driving around was for friends and fun. There are many adults who never get over this conditioned behavior. Instead, at a time of incredible competition, information overload and obsolescence of knowledge, they are still floating through life, driving around, failing to take advantage of one of the very best learning methodologies ever discovered.

Don't let this happen to you. Never let your car be running without educational audio programs playing. Make every minute count. One great idea or technique can change the course of your career and dramatically increase your income.

Express Gratitude: Fill your mind with gratitude instead of negative news programs. All the successful people I've studied and have been around practice gratitude. The best entrepreneurs, the best athletes, and the best parents practice gratitude. While most are worried about economic crisis and turmoil, the top 1% are thinking about what they are grateful for and what opportunities lay ahead. They also ask, "What's good about this crisis?" Imagine how different your thoughts and action would be if you were consistently focusing on the positive, being grateful, and seeing opportunity instead of getting stuck in negativity.

What can you do to make sure you're sparking your mind daily?

_____

_____

_____

_____

_____

2. They get active and increase the strength of their bodies.

Walk around the block, do 20 push-ups daily, go for a jog. Don't neglect working out and don't neglect your body because when you feel strong physically, you will feel stronger mentally. Just 10 minutes or more of quick exercise is enough to stimulate the receptors in your brain. Focus on progress, not perfection. Start with 10 minutes each morning, then go to 15, then go to 20. Go from three days per week and work up to five days per week. Just make sure you're sparking your body consistently.

3. They reach out to those playing the game at a higher level.

I've dedicated an entire chapter to this subject and for good reason. Even those already making millions can learn from those who are operating at a higher level. You must stay humble, but never lose your hunger. Anyone who's achieved greatness has had a role model and mentor to challenge them.

When you talk with people playing the game at a higher level than you, they can help you see challenges and opportunities you might not be able to see. You don't know what you don't know, and there is nothing more motivating than feeling your awareness, intelligence, and perspective growing. Those living at a world class level are always striving to become better, setting bigger goals, and reaching for new heights. Continue challenging yourself, and don't stop. Self-made billionaire Richard Branson was asked what his motivation was and he said:

> *"I keep challenging myself. I see life almost like one long university education that I never had—every day I'm learning something new."*

When you stop growing you die. You're either progressing towards your goals or falling behind. There is no in-between. Make a commitment to become a lifelong student of the game and you'll never have to worry about complacency again. Here's one of the most important questions you could ever ask yourself:

What could you do the rest of your life that would keep you fascinated and engaged?

_____

_____

_____

_____

_____

CHAPTER

13

NOW MATTERS

"The wealthiest place on the planet is the cemetery, because it's filled with brilliant ideas, potential, all wasted."

— Tony Robbins

If I didn't tell myself NOW mattered, this book wouldn't have been written for a couple more years, if ever. One of the main reasons people aren't achieving the success they're truly capable of is they've never told themselves NOW matters. This 'someday' mentality is killing so many dreams and goals. In fact, I'd say it's near the top of the list of reasons why our society is filled with regret, frustration, stress, and unfulfilled potential.

If you want real change, you must change something you do daily and adopt this perspective right away. There will never be a right time and if you're waiting for the perfect time, you'll be waiting for a long time. There is NO tomorrow for champions and you'll find urgency evident in every leader. In a conversation I had with motivational speaker and visionary Eric Thomas, he stated his No. 1 focus was to seize each day.

If you take care of today, tomorrow takes care of itself. If you take care of your days, your weeks take care of themselves. If you take care of your weeks, your months take care of themselves. If you take care of your months, your years are exceptional. I'm confidently assuming you're ready to make quantum leaps in your life. Here's how you start. Make the most of today, then tomorrow, then the next day. Most people spend the first half of their life saying they're too young and the second half saying they're too old.

I'm guessing you'd like to be financially free by the time you're 65 years old? I'm sure everybody does. Unfortunately, that's not reality.

At age 65, as reported by the Social Security Board in Washington, D.C.:

- 69% of American people are dependent on relatives, friends, or charities.

- 29% are still working.

- 2% are financially independent.

I will tell you becoming that 2% starts with urgency, and you MUST have a sense of urgency if you're serious about success. Do you think those struggling in their 30s, 40s, and 50s told themselves they were going to struggle when they were older? Of course not. If you talked to them when they were younger, they were confident they would have their dream house, dream job, have lots of money, and be enjoying life to the fullest. What happened? They never told themselves NOW matters and they didn't connect their daily actions with their future goals. Don't fall into the same trap.

The people who will be unstoppable over the next two to five years have a vision to live differently than those around them. They have a strong vision for the path less traveled, a vision for the extraordinary life, financial freedom, flexible lifestyle, and ultimately, a fulfilled life. The vision isn't enough on its own. You must have a sense of urgency and attach everything you're doing to your future self. The time is NOW and it's time to take full responsibility for your future. If you want success bad enough, you'll find a way to create it. Opportunities are only opportunities if you're taking full advantage of them. I've laid out a simple framework for you to follow, but now you must own it. It won't be easy, but if you take it day by day, you'll start to see real progress. Progress is a great motivator.

I hope this book has opened your eyes to what's possible for you. I hope it's given you clarity on how to achieve the success you want. Our economy is in desperate need of leaders, so take it upon yourself to become the best version of yourself. If you don't have a plan for building a great life, you will fall into someone else's plan! Guess what they have planned for you? Not much. It's how you're living daily that either makes you unstoppable or stresses you out, so approach every day with confidence and intention and never forget that the only limitations you have are those you place on yourself. Make a concrete decision that you're going to be the best person you possibly can be for those around you, and for yourself.

Since 2008, when I made the decision to never settle for mediocrity, life has never been the same. A decision means to cut away ALL alternatives, leaving you no other options but to succeed. There has never been a better time in human history to create, design, craft, build, and live the lifestyle you dream of. I strongly urge you to find a community of like-minded people you can connect with on a regular basis, a community of people with similar goals and ambitions as you. Being around those who can elevate your standards, hold you accountable, and challenge your thinking is priceless.

Are you ready to start elevating your game? Are you ready to tell your boss you quit? Are you ready to start that business that creates financial freedom for you and your family? Well good, but that's not enough. Now comes the part most people forget:

Implementation. This is the moment of truth—the moment when you decide to get in the game or remain on the sidelines. Reading this book to elevate your perspective, raise your standards, and rebuild your belief system is a great first step, but it is just that, a first step. The key is to make sure that it's not your last step. It will take a lot of hard work and focus to maintain the motivation and drive for your big ambitions and vision to become a reality. It will take even more work and discipline to stick with it for more than just a few days or weeks. But at the end of the day, all that matters is your answer to this question:

Do you want to be living an exceptional life on your terms with flexibility and freedom, or do you want to build somebody else's dream, instead?

If you're not up for the challenge, then do what most people do after they read a book that has the potential to change their lives—nothing. Put this book down and forget everything I've taught you and continue your life as it exists today. Hide behind excuses like, "It's too hard," "I don't have enough money to get started," or, "I'll get started tomorrow"—and go on collecting paychecks or searching for a 'real' job. If you've made it this far, I know that's not you. I want to end with a story that illustrates the power of adopting the right perspective.

Change Your Perspective, Change Your Life.

There were two boys who were being raised by a single dad. The dad was trying his best to make ends meet. As you may or may not know, raising two kids can be a challenging task and it's even tougher trying to do everything by yourself. He was doing everything he could to provide for his boys, but kept falling further and further behind. The pressure and demands of being a single dad kept piling up and in the heat of the moment he snapped and made a decision that would change his family's life forever. One late evening, desperate for money, he decided to rob a local convenience store.

The store clerk, along with a mother of three, ended up getting shot. After a court hearing he was sentenced to life in prison. Both his kids ended up going to different qualified foster homes. The unimaginable had happened. They lost both parents. Years went by and the brothers had very different futures. One became extremely successful, ran his own business, and was living the american dream. The other was in and out of jail, got addicted to drugs, and lived a life of struggle. A journalist was very intrigued and interested about what had happened to the boys. She decided to follow up with them to possibly create a story. She caught up with both boys 15 years later and asked them both the same question:

How did your life end up the way it did?

They both, ironically, had the same answer: "With a father like mine, how else would my life turn out?" Same tragic past, but different perspectives, and with different perspectives come different outcomes. I don't care what situation you are in, what part of town you are from, or how your last six months have gone. Your past has nothing to do with your future, but your current decisions do. How you respond to what happens is everything. So from this moment on, make the conscious decision to become the best version of yourself.

CHAPTER

14

I CHALLENGE YOU!

"If it doesn't challenge you, it won't change you"

— Fred Devito

There are only two things that can change your life and business:

- Something good or bad comes into your life.

- Something new comes from within you.

Waiting for something good to come into your life could take time, and you don't have that. I'd recommend finding something within you. I hope this book has urged you to stop playing small with your gifts, talents, and dreams, and to start experiencing life at a level 10. If somebody is out earning or achieving at a higher level than you, they are just amplifying more of themselves. They are showing up in a different way than you are, but that ends now. I was serious when I said this book will change your life and I want to prove it to you. We're going on a 30 day challenge and the only way to see a big shift in your results is total immersion, which means going all in. As the economy gets worse, I want you to dominate and to dominate you must get addicted to giving your all. You've learned now that anything is possible with total dedication and commitment.

For the next 30 days, you're going on a money making vacation and when YOU change, everything will change for YOU. Get serious about your biggest ambitions and who you must become to accomplish them. Remember, doing the same thing and expecting different results is the definition of insanity.

There are two types of people in this world. Those who will do whatever it takes to create the life of their dreams... and everybody else. Choose who you want to become very wisely.

THE 30 DAY CHALLENGE

Download The Free 6-Month Blueprint PDF at:
www.PeterJVoogd.com/bonuses

Today's Date:_____   Goal Date: _____

What are the top five goals you want to accomplish within the next 30 days?

    1. _____

    2. _____

    3. _____

    4. _____

    5. _____

Break down what you must do weekly to make sure you accomplish your 30 day goals:

    Week 1 Top 3:

    1. _____

    2. _____

    3. _____

    Week 1 Reward:_____

Week 2 Top 3:

1. _____

2. _____

3. _____

Week 2 Reward:_____

Week 3 Top 3:

1. _____

2. _____

3. _____

Week 3 Reward:_____

Week 4 Top 3:

1. _____

2. _____

3. _____

Week 4 Reward:_____

How are you going to feel once your 30 day challenge is over? It's important for you to visualize with deep precision the feelings you're going to experience at the end of your 30 day challenge.

_____

_____

_____

_____

_____

_____

_____

_____

_____

_____

Starting Today:

What are the key behaviors needed to accomplish your 30-day goals?

    1. _____

    2. _____

    3. _____

What are your weekly rituals that must happen no matter what? (Refer to Chapter 11)

    1. _____

    2. _____

    3. _____

What are you going to ***start*** doing today that's congruent with your 30 day challenge goals?

_____

_____

_____

_____

_____

What do you need to **_stop_** doing today that's not aligned with your Big 5, holding you back, or killing your current progress or momentum?

_____

_____

_____

_____

_____

What are you going to **_continue_** to do that's been serving you well?

_____

_____

_____

_____

_____

Signature _____   Date _____

I challenge you to take these questions seriously and become more intentional in all you do. I can assure you _Wealth_, _Lifestyle_, and _Freedom_ are best experienced at a young age! Are you really living your potential, expressing your creative genius, and living an inspiring life? You're just as capable and deserving as everybody else, but understand it takes massive sacrifice along with implementation of the right actions.

This is the greatest time in human history for those who take 100% responsibility for their economic well-being. Commit to these tactics with the focus that your life deserves and continue to cement in your mind that you are always in control of your economy, regardless of the outside circumstances. Respect to you and the progress you're making towards a world class life. I'm here for you, and once you complete this 30-day challenge, please share your success story personally with me at: Peter@PeterJVoogd.com.

Help spread the word about the *6 Months to 6 Figures* Movement and stay in the know: Follow me on Twitter @PeterVoogd23 and friend me on Facebook www.facebook.com/PeterVoogd23.

I love connecting with like-minded people like you.

As a thank you for purchasing *6 Months to 6 Figures* and committing yourself to excellence, building a business that matters, and taking control of your future, I've assembled a series of valuable tools you can use to help maximize your entrepreneurial experience. Sure, I could have offered you some BS special report or free video seminar like most 'online marketers,' but I'd rather give you something practical that will help you move your business forward and get you on the path to making immediate income.

You can claim the $785 worth of free resources at:

www.PeterJVoogd.com/bonuses

Game Changers Academy:
The Elite Mastermind Community
For Entrepreneurs

I'm blessed, and blown away, to say that over 250,000 people have now read this book.

I want to <u>thank you</u> for being one of those readers.

Every single day I get messages from people all around the world, from young entrepreneurs to seasoned CEO's and everything in between. They tell me how they've applied what they learned in this book, how it's improved their life and these stories light me up.

However, one common thread tends to runs through the messages I receive... **the desire for more**.

Which doesn't surprise me given the changes in the economy and the ever-growing realization that life *can* be lived on your own terms. Once you get a taste of how life *can* be, you aren't just hungry for more... you crave it.

More expanded training, more connections with like-minded people, more resources and the exact action plans and one-on-one answers of how to implement everything you just learned in this book.

You talked, so I listened.

My team and I have taken each and every concept, insight and strategy in this book to a whole new level. Instead of covering just the surface, we drilled deep, down to the core. From this we built an exact action plan and system anyone can follow, step by step, to elevate themselves and their business to new heights.

It's an utterly unique entrepreneurial experience, which I know is a bold claim. However when you peek behind the curtain, you'll see why I can say it with complete confidence.

Right now we have a thriving community of success-seekers building their own *6 Months to 6 Figures* (and even 7-figures) success story, and I want you to join us.

If you're ready to stop accepting the cards you were dealt and you are truly dedicated to your success, then I'd like to invite you inside our prestigious Game Changers Academy mastermind training & community. This is the complete system you need to thrive in this new economy.

Visit www.GameChangersAcdemy.com/apply right now to apply to join this elite community.

I want to be very clear; this is not for everyone. If you don't deeply desire prosperity, freedom and having the ability to escape the norm, you'll not like what you see inside this mastermind and training program. I don't hold anything back and I'll break some dearly held myths of yours.

However, if you're looking for the right mindset, skills, strategies, habits, support, answers, community, million dollar network, and step-by-step systems to create your ideal lifestyle and income, quicker than you can ever imagine, then you'll find yourself welcome in The Game Changers Academy.

There are thousands that have proven themselves ready for the next level and the results are amazing. I have received countless success stories of people who have quit their jobs they hated, doubled their income in a month, built million dollar businesses, and much more.

"Thanks for being an incredible inspiration and leader for me. Mastering 6 Months to 6 Figures helped me hit my goal of "6 months to 6 figures", quit my day job and actualize my dreams. I am forever grateful and indebted to you and your work. Fan for life." – Adrienne D.

"After going through 6 Months to 6 Figures, I began reaching out to mentors/people playing the game at a higher level than me daily. Within a month I had two six-figure mentors and a multiple seven-figure mentor. Fast-forward to today - my income has literally 10x'ed and I am now making $10,000+ per month.

Crazy what a change 3 months can have." – Edward B.

People are getting real results in the real world. Even with the challenges that life brings:

"Where I was doing okay last year making $150k a year with my previous company, I gave away my shares to start a new company that is now doing well over seven figures in profit within 12 months... while fighting for custody over my son, and going through a very lengthy and nasty divorce.

It was a long and difficult ride but very much worth it and I want to thank you. I could write a whole book with examples but again, thanks." – Van D.

That's just a quick insight into the level we play the game at.

Imagine what's possible if you applied your drive and determination to a proven system with support from hundreds of other success-seekers. Does that scare you, or motivate you?

I challenge you to stop the excuses, quit the BS and to finally take control of your future. If you accept, visit:

www.GameChangersMovement.com/apply

Bonus Resources:

www.PeterJVoogd.com — Helping you live life on YOUR terms. We are focused on bringing you new, relevant and powerful resources to help you thrive as an entrepreneur. Here you can check out my podcast and other great resources to guide you.

www.GameChangersMovement.com — The premier mastermind program and community for entrepreneurs and professionals. As featured on Forbes, Entrepreneur.com, Business Insider, and more. This is the all-in-one system you need to absolutely thrive as an entrepreneur, sales professional or marketer. We have a vibrant community of Game Changers from all throughout the world that is growing fast. Change your Circle of Influence and come join the movement.

www.6M6F.com — You asked for it, now you get it. We have taken this book to a whole new level and have created a step-by-step system and community for those that are ready to make 6 Months to 6 Figures a reality. Join our elite community and get everything you need to succeed in our one-stop program.

www.YoungAmbition.co — Lifestyle clothing for those who embrace being different and have a hunger to become the best.

Also, feel free to email me at:
Peter@PeterJVoogd.com
for special requests such
as bulk purchases of
6 Months to 6 Figures
for your company, sales team,
friends, and family!

ABOUT THE AUTHOR:
PETER VOOGD

A visionary, game changer, speaker, author, mentor, and dedicated entrepreneur, Peter Voogd is on a mission to shift our culture, and won't stop until his vision becomes a reality. Peter can't stand traditional education, and feels our society isn't doing enough to educate, teach, and train our youth on how to REALLY thrive in this tough economy. He's taken it upon himself to guide and educate our Millennials on what it takes to not only succeed, but THRIVE! Peter's strategies have been featured in *Entrepreneur Magazine, Forbes, Huffington Post, Business Insider, Yahoo Small Business, Yahoo Finance, MSN*, SUCCESS and many other international publications.

Peter has seen a lot of success over the years, but even more failure. He's used his past to design his ideal future, and has dedicated the last 10 years to helping people maximize their potential. He's been labeled as the leading authority for Millennials and one of the top influencers to follow along with Tony Robbins, Gary Vaynerchuk and more. He has an authentic, raw understanding of what it takes to motivate and inspire. He's trained and led over 6,000 Entrepreneurs, Sales Professionals, Managers, College Students, Young Professionals, Business Owners, Olympians and many others to high levels of success.

He started his first business when he was 15, and found himself broke, stressed and discouraged by the age of 22. By 23, he had made his first 6-figure income, and 3 1/2 years later his earnings were over $1 million. He then took the same formula and applied it in another industry, and has dedicated himself to teaching it to others so they don't make the same mistakes he did. Despite the challenge of lacking training, Peter became the fastest manager to reach $1 million in annual sales in his company's 60 + year history, but left his 6 figure income because the magnitude of his mission was growing. He strongly believes the more people you help to succeed, the more successful you become.

Peter has started a few movements to empower and train entrepreneurs and young professionals called *The Game Changers Academy* as well as the program driven from this book, *6 Months to 6 Figures* (see more at www.PeterJVoogd.com). Both have quickly become some of the most prestigious training and networking communities in the world, and continue to attract ambitious professionals and entrepreneurs from all over the world. He understands on a deep level that entrepreneurs are the driving force and future of our society.

He is also the Founder of one of iTunes top podcasts, "*The Young Entrepreneur Lifestyle Podcast,*" which is focused on bringing results, guidance, and excellence to entrepreneurs worldwide. It's helping entrepreneurs do business and live life on their terms.

Learn more at: www.peterjvoogd.com/podcast

Connect with Peter on social media:

Facebook	:	PeterJVoogd
LinkedIn	:	Peter Voogd
Twitter	:	PeterVoogd23
Instagram	:	PeterJVoogd
Snapchat	:	Ambition23
Google+	:	Peter Voogd
Email	:	Peter@PeterJVoogd.com
Facebook Group	:	Facebook.com/groups/SixMonthsToSixFigures

OTHER BOOKS BY PETER VOOGD:

The Entrepreneur's Blueprint to Massive Success --
*How to Create an Exceptional Lifestyle While Doing
Business on **YOUR** Terms"*

Available now on Amazon:
www.amazon.com/dp/B010OTE1DI/

BOOK PETER TO SPEAK

Peter is now one of the top Millennial motivational speakers in the world. Book him to speak at your event or company.

Peter Voogd has been engaging and inspiring audiences for more than nine years, and has helped thousands with his dynamic and result-oriented messages. He has been in the top 1% of performers in every industry he's been in. This has given him the unique position of sitting down with the leading experts on human performance and achievement, as well as many top CEOs, revolutionary entrepreneurs, exceptional athletes, entertainers and Olympic champions, to uncover and share the success secrets behind their extraordinary achievements. Peter has organized what he's learned into a framework that creates breakthroughs in sales teams, companies, and professionals worldwide. Peter can relate to his audiences at a level most can't, which is why he is one of the most requested speakers in the industry.

Peter has spoken to companies like Ford Motors, Cutco, Berkshire Hathaway, Thrive, Explore Talent, Vemma, World Ventures, Avon, and many other direct sales and international sales companies.

"Peter's highly valued, actionable and results-oriented content, along with his confident, and engaging style has made him one of the most requested speakers in the industry. Peter has real knowledge, and an authentic, raw understanding of what it takes to motivate at the highest level. He knows how to inspire, create real change, and raise the standards of every audience he comes in contact with.
He is known for dealing in reality, and has a unique combination of humor and stories to penetrate his audiences."

Isaac Tolpin,
CEO ChooseGrowth.com

4

SOME OF MY FAVORITE QUOTES

"Discipline Creates Lifestyle"
– Peter Voogd

"Think Like a Millionaire, Hustle Like You're Broke"
– Peter Voogd

"Respect people who find time for you in their busy schedule,
but love the people who never look at their schedule
when you need them."
– Unknown

"Sometimes not getting what you want is the best thing
that could ever happen to you."
– Peter Voogd

"A successful man is one who can lay a firm foundation
with the bricks others have thrown at him."
– Jordan Wirsz

"Instead of wondering when your next vacation is, maybe you
should set up a lifestyle you don't need to escape from."
– Seth Godin

"Your time is limited, so don't waste it living someone else's life."
– Steve Jobs

*"When you judge another person,
you're not defining them;
you're defining yourself."*
– Peter Voogd

*"You must design your ideal future,
it won't just show up."*
– Peter Voogd

*"People who develop themselves daily, don't
participate in recessions."*
– Peter Voogd

*"Never let someone who gave up on their dreams
talk you out of yours."*
– Peter Voogd

*"If your presence doesn't make an impact,
your absence won't make a difference."*
– Peter Voogd

*"Never let the things you want make you
forget the things you have. Stay grateful."*
– Peter Voogd

ACKNOWLEDGEMENTS

I don't know where to start because I've been blessed with a long list of great people that have stood by my side. I believe the only things that really change your life are the experiences you create and the people you meet along the way. I've met some amazing people on my journey to a meaningful and impactful life. It's going to be impossible to thank everybody who's helped me, and it would take a couple chapters! I'll try my best.

My mom and dad have played the key roles in my success, and have always let me be who I wanted to be. They gave me the ultimate gift: "Belief in myself." Words can't describe how much it means to have parents who let you be who you want, not who they want you to be. Thanks Mom and Dad, I love you. My brother, Chris, for putting up with me his entire life, and I can only imagine how tough it was being my younger brother. You're a true leader, and someone who can accomplish anything you put your mind to. I am very proud of the man you've become, and you have a very bright future in front of you. You've attracted a great woman in Tia, and you're raising an intelligent and strong boy in Kaii. My cousins, Ben, Melissa and Stacie, who I've grown up with and have endless memories with. So proud of how strong willed, independent, and driven you all are. My amazing girlfriend, Kayla, who has played a significant role in who I've become, and what I've been able to do. You've been there through thick and thin, and have always supported me 100%, believed in me, and trusted my vision. You've taught me the power of patience, and often remind me to enjoy the journey. My love for you grows daily, and I couldn't have found a better other half. I'm very proud of you, and I appreciate everything you've done for me. As far as business goes, I've had numerous people that have played a role in my early success. The first person that comes to mind is Isaac Tolpin, my first official mentor. There is no way I'd be where I am today without his guidance, wisdom, and different way of thinking. He taught me the power of "taking few opinions," "thinking different," and always "choosing growth," in the moment. Some of the most powerful and meaningful conversations I've ever had have been with Isaac. He's a prime example of practicing what you preach, and living a truly purposeful and meaningful life. Thanks for all you do, and for never trying to manage me, but leading me instead.

My Vector family. First, Jeremy Bell for being one of the first people to inspire me to think bigger. You showed me it was possible to own multiple homes at a young age, and watching you get $40k bonus checks kept me inspired when I was starting out. Isaac Stegman for being one of my first mentors, and for teaching me the fundamentals of success and achievement when I was starting out. You had a huge impact on my early success in direct sales. More than most realize. John Bedford for making me a better leader, and for bringing out the best in me. You're a fierce competitor and somebody who I respect at the highest level. I wouldn't have reached the heights I did if it wasn't for you pushing the envelope first. Zac Beckhusen for being crazy enough to take almost a dozen trips a year with me. You're one of the most fun dudes to hang out with, but more importantly, you're authentic and genuine. PJ Potter for being a strong leader and pushing me past what I thought I was capable of. You taught me to be soft on people but tough on results, and that's a lesson I'll take with me forever. You engrained in me how important integrity and character is, and I appreciate you deeply for that. Karl Gedris for showing me how to build a Dynasty the right way, and for always pushing the envelope. Amber Martindale for pushing me beyond my limits, and always leading by example. Your passion is very inspiring. Will Burdette for recruiting me into direct sales, and always believing in my abilities and ambition. You knew exactly how to work with me, and I admire how simplistic you've made your life. When I was struggling in 2008, and felt like I had no hope I reached out to sales champion and mentor Hal Elrod. I invested all the money I had so I could coach with him, Jon Berghoff, and Jon Vroman. It was one of the best decisions I've ever made in my life. Since then, Hal has becomes a dear friend, my mastermind partner, and is like the older brother I never had. He was such a good salesman, he talked me into moving to Southern

California, just a couple of miles away from him.

Once I realized how powerful mentorship was, and how crucial it was to increased results, I reached out to multi-millionaire and business extraordinaire Jordan Wirsz. Jordan has shifted my thinking and heightened my perspective at such an extreme level. When I told him I had $125,000 saved by age 23, he laughed and said, "You think that's a lot?" Much respect to Jordan for raising my standards and for the timeless wisdom he continues to share with me. When it comes to pure results, Jordan's had the biggest impact. I will share a lot of what Jordan taught me throughout this book.

When I was transitioning between careers and felt my mission growing I reached out to Gary Vaynerchuk, who took interest in me. We've had numerous conversations, but our first stands out the most. One forty-five minute conversation can change your life! Gary expressed the importance of reverse engineering your success by creating your ideal outcome and then working backwards to create a plan to achieve it. He also shared the importance of focusing on your legacy, and realizing that everything you do is part of that. Appreciate all blunt insight, and the time you've given me GV. Thanks to Honoree Corder for leading by example, and staying massively productive in all you do. The way you work, how much you get done, and what you've accomplished is very inspiring to me. James Malinchak for sharing with me it's not about working harder or smarter, but working right. You're one of the most strategic and brilliant thinkers I know. I wanted to appreciate Hugo Fernandez for designing the cover of this book, and going the extra mile to make sure our brand is top notch. You're one of the most talented, ambitious, intelligent young hustlers I know. It's been a pleasure helping you on your journey towards massive success and impact.

There have been many more people who have impacted my success along the way, and I sincerely appreciate every one of you. If I missed you, I sincerely apologize but know I am grateful for you.

ONE LAST THING

May I ask you for a favor?

If you got anything out of this book, if you took notes, if it shifted your thinking or inspired you at all, I'm hoping you'll do something for me.

Give a copy to somebody else.

Ask them to read it. Let them know what's possible for them if they start to value their dreams and goals over their excuses.

We need them. We need you. Spread the word.

Thank you.

Peter Voogd

74878523R00100

Made in the USA
San Bernardino, CA
22 April 2018